THE
Woman's Day
BOOK OF
Household Hints

THE
Woman's Day
BOOK OF
Household Hints

EDITED BY

Martha Ellen Hughes

WILLIAM MORROW AND COMPANY, INC.
NEW YORK   1978

Library of Congress Cataloging in Publication Data
Main entry under title:

The *Woman's Day* book of household hints.

    1. Home economics. I. Hughes, Martha Ellen. II. Woman's day. III. Title: Book of household hints.
TX158.W58   640   77-25318
ISBN 0-688-03283-4

BOOK DESIGN   JOHN P. BALL

Printed in the United States of America.

3   4   5   6   7   8   9   10

Contents

Introduction   9

1. Cleaning and Housework   13

    General Housework   15
    In the Laundry Room: Washing,
        Drying and Ironing   18
    Windows, Walls, Curtains and
        Upholstery   24
    Spots, Stains and Odors   26
    Clean-up Catchall   28

2. Home Organization and Storage   31

    Clothes and Accessories   33
    In the Kitchen   36
    In a Child's Room   38
    . . . and All Around the House   40

3. Kitchen Hints   45

    General, Storage and Shopping   47
    Dishwashing and Defrosting   50
    Kitchen Catchall: Cooking Techniques
        and Food Ideas   52
    Meats, Poultry and Fish   58
    Potatoes, Rice, Breads and Grain   63
    Eggs, Butter and Cheese   67
    Vegetables and Salads   69
    Fruits   75
    Cakes, Cookies, Pies and Desserts   78

4. Handyman's Hints and Home Repairs   85

   Painting and Plastering   87
   General Hints   88

5. Gardening   93

   Indoor Plants and Flowers   95
   Outdoor Gardening   98
   Backyard Bird Watching   104

6. Home Sewing   107

   General Sewing Hints   109
   Mending Techniques   115
   Recycling Clothes   118

7. Needlework, Crafts and Decorating Ideas 123

   Yarn, Thread and Embroidery   125
   Knitting and Crochet   127
   Quilting and Patchwork   131
   Rugmaking   133
   Crafts and Decorating Ideas   135

8. For Special Occasions   141

   Baby Showers and New Arrivals   143
   Birthdays   145
   Bridal Showers,
      Weddings and Anniversaries   148
   Christmas, Holidays and
      Holiday Gift-Giving   152
   Easter   155
   Halloween   156
   General Hints for Parties and
      Gift-Giving, Decorating and
      Gift Wrapping   157

9. Travel Tips 161

    Motor Trips and Car Hints 163
    Camping and Cooking at the Campsite 165
    Traveling with Children 168

10. Raising Children 171

    Family Harmony and Togetherness 173
    Eating 179
    Sleeping 181
    Bathing, Grooming and Dressing 183
    Child Safety 186
    Schoolwork, Learning and the Value
      of Money 188
    Encouraging Play 193
    Art 196
    Toys to Make 197
    Kids' Catchall 201

11. For Those in Need 203

    Sick Children 205
    The Elderly and the Handicapped 207
    Hospital Patients 210
    Medical Catchall 211

12. Personal Hygiene and Grooming Tips 213

13. Money Matters and Budgeting 217

14. Miscellaneous Hints 223

    Index 233

Introduction

On October 7, 1937, when the United States was eight years into the Great Depression, the first issue of *Woman's Day* appeared in response to the great need for a service magazine that would help homemakers during times of scarcity.

In its first issue, the editors openly appealed to their readers to share advice with their neighbors: How were they, *personally*, coping with the times, most especially the nationwide scarcity of food and the infectiously low morale? The response was overwhelming. Letters poured in from all over the country and the "Neighbors" column, from which the household hints in this book have been adapted, became and still is today one of the most popular and practical features of *Woman's Day*.

With the outbreak of World War II, the editorial focus of the magazine was expanded to include articles on dealing with other shortages, economizing, and do-it-yourself projects. In the "Neighbors" column, readers offered solutions for stretching rationed food supplies as well as for dealing with the widespread deficiency of commonplace materials.

Today, forty years after its inception, *Woman's Day* continues to reflect the changing needs of its readers. But the basic feeling which initially prompted the editors of the "Neighbors" column to call upon their readers for suggestions remains unchanged: "Running a home and caring for a family successfully is one of the hardest jobs in the world. . . . Maybe we can get together and help make this job easier. . . . Perhaps we can make every woman's day a little easier."

This book, then, is a collection of the 1,001 best hints—for homemakers, from homemakers—chosen from countless letters published in "Neighbors." The information from each letter has been rewritten to provide easy, quick reference, and the hints have been organized by subject matter into fourteen main categories: Cleaning and Housework; Home Organization and Storage; Kitchen Hints; Handyman's Hints and Home Repairs; Gardening; Home Sewing; Needlework, Crafts and Decorating Ideas; For Special Occasions; Travel Tips; Raising Children; For Those in Need; Personal Hygiene and Grooming Tips; Money Matters and Budgeting; and Miscellaneous Hints.

The book offers many time-honored tips that have been passed down within families for generations, as well as ideas from readers whose sudden inspirations have paid off. While the personal tone of the letters has been removed, the remarkable ingenuity of the women who wrote them shines through today as it did when they were first shared in *Woman's Day*.

THE
Woman's Day
BOOK OF
Household Hints

1.

Cleaning and Housework

General Housework

Make a disposable apron for dirty chores such as cleaning ovens, frying foods, washing dogs or feeding babies. Cut holes for the neck and arms in a large plastic garbage-can liner and wear as an apron.

❀

A roomy "clothespin" apron worn when cleaning house is a real step-saver. Use the pockets to hold picked-up odds and ends that you can return to their proper place as you work.

❀

Wear fabric gloves under rubber gloves. The fabric absorbs perspiration, makes the rubber gloves easier to pull on and off, and acts as an insulator.

❀

If the house is in a mess and guests telephone at the last minute to say they are on the way, there are many tricks for making the house orderly in seconds. In the living room, stick all litter under couches and chairs. Shake out throw rugs and put over dirty spots in carpet. Wrap a towel around your arm and slide it quickly over furniture tops. In the kitchen, stack the dirty dishes in the cupboards; wipe off counters; sweep the dirt off the floor into the broom closet. Set out coffee cups, dishes, whatever will be necessary for entertaining, so that you will not have to open cupboards to reveal your secrets. In the bathroom, close the curtains around the tub and put all dirty clothes in the bathtub. Close bedroom doors. Sit back and wait for the doorbell to ring.

❄

An energy-saving trick for doing housework is to alternate hard tasks with easy ones. Start with something strenuous, such as weeding the garden; then tackle a quiet job in the house, such as mending. If you have been standing up to iron, make the next task a sitting-down one. Alternating energy levels is a proven reenergizer.

❄

When housecleaning with small children around, have them stage a talent show for you—singing songs, reciting poems or telling stories from their favorite books. This speeds up the chores, avoids crankiness and keeps little hands out of trouble.

❄

During the summer, lift your spirits by taking household chores outside. There is no rule against polishing silverware, washing children's hair, or ironing clothes (provided you have an extension cord) in the backyard.

❄

To boost morale while doing housework, try wearing "cleaning costumes"—crazy outfits which you wouldn't normally have the courage to wear out of the house.

❄

Keep a notebook to record anything that sparks your interest—a new recipe, a new craft, a new way to brighten a room, etc. On days when the idea of doing housework makes you want to run the other way, refer to your notebook and set aside an hour or two to begin a new project. You'll feel refreshed and energetic and get through the routine chores in half the time!

❀

Instead of spending several tedious days in a row cleaning the kitchen, do the work piecemeal. After washing breakfast or lunch dishes, empty one drawer or shelf and use the soapy dishwater to clean it thoroughly.

❀

Avoid the spring cleaning rush by sorting out bureau drawers the first part of February.

❀

To clean such things as dresser drawers or sewing kits without disturbing the contents, cover the vacuum cleaner nozzle with cheesecloth held in place by a rubber band.

❀

Use a toy dustmop instead of a feather duster—it's easier to get at hard-to-reach shelves and the mop collects dust instead of scattering it.

In the Laundry Room: Washing, Drying and Ironing

Washing and Drying

Use an old Bathinette in the laundry room. Soak clothes in the tub; fold and sort clothes on the table top; when ironing, hang clothes on hangers from the crossbars. In the small pockets of the Bathinette, put a mending kit, cleaning fluid, spray starch and other items.

❀

Save all tags and labels off garments, plus receipts, and pin to a bulletin board near your washer for special laundering instructions. If something turns out unsatisfactory, return it to the store and ask for a refund; get the manufacturer's address and write to complain. Most stores and manufacturers encourage customer response.

❀

In winter, hang wet clothes in the basement, rather than using the dryer. This not only saves on utility bills, but the damp clothes humidify the house.

❀

Before putting clothes in the washer, button dresses, shirts, etc., and turn them inside out. Fewer buttons will be lost and there will be less fading on the right side of the garments.

❀

To facilitate the drying of hand-washed articles, put them in the washing machine with the control set halfway through the last "spin" or "dry" setting and spin out the water. The garments will dry in a much shorter time than the old "squeeze and knead" method.

❀

An old window-screen frame covered with fiber glass screening makes a good flat drying surface for sweaters.

❀

To shorten the drying time for blankets, pin them to the clothesline by top and bottom hems, then crumple brown wrapping paper into several loose balls and place these at intervals within the fold.

❀

An inexpensive and easily stored drying rack for lingerie and other small items can be made from an old umbrella. Simply remove the fabric from the frame, bind any rough edges with tape, and hang by the handle.

❀

When hanging rugs on the line on a windy day, pin front and back halves together with clothespins that have been placed partway down sides; the rugs will blow freely, yet will stay put.

❀

When children's snowsuits get wet, dirty and muddied, eliminate the need of washing them through the winter: Let the snowsuits dry out thoroughly, then use a vacuum cleaner attachment to brush loose and take out the dirt.

❄

To dry wet mittens in half the time it usually takes, pull each one over the bottom of a small jar and stand the open ends of the jars on a radiator.

❄

Instead of sliding the clothespin bag along as you pin wet clothes on the line, tie an old belt on the bag and hang it over your shoulder.

❄

If lint from the automatic washer is clogging the drain, tie an old nylon stocking over the end of the washer outlet hose. Extend the stocking foot over the end of the hose, so that the water drains easily. Tightly tie a piece of wire around the stocking to secure it to the hose.

❄

To remove lint, put a yard of nylon netting into the dryer with wet clothes; use white net for light clothes, dark for dark clothes.

❄

Whiten linen or cotton by boiling in a solution of three parts water and one part cream of tartar.

Ironing

For washing and ironing ruffled crocheted doilies, follow this procedure: Wash and starch the doily, using old-fashioned hot starch, if available. When dried to a damp stage, iron the doily lightly; it will still be slightly damp. Set a plate on a tall jar, and invert the doily over the plate. Let stand until thoroughly dry: the ruffle will be crimped beautifully.

❀

Use a child's crib as an ironing aid: Take the hardware off the spare side and hook it to the wall, with the slats horizontal, near the ironing board. Hang tablecloths, napkins, sheets and linens on it after ironing. Use also to store linens—simply cover the crib side with plastic sheeting.

❀

Iron the top part of pants on the wrong side, then turn to the right side for the legs. The pockets and waistband will have a smoother look.

❀

Instead of ironing pajamas, blue jeans, dish towels, sheets and pillowcases, just fold neatly, stack on a chair, and sit on them while ironing other things.

❀

To clean a stainless steel iron, first preheat it to lowest setting and unplug; spray with "warm oven" cleaner and wait five minutes; wipe with damp sponge.

❀

Eliminate a newly-let-down hemline or perk up a permanent-press garment that has lost its crisp finish by sprinkling with a solution of one part white vinegar to one part water before pressing the piece. The freshened appearance will last through many washings.

❀

To prevent creases made by hanging garments over a wire hanger, slice an empty paper-towel roll the long way, fit it over the bottom wire of the hanger and tape the slit.

❀

To keep articles such as shirt sleeves from dragging on the floor when you are ironing, slip an opened card table under the narrow end of your ironing board.

❀

Keep an old pair of scissors near your ironing board so loose threads or ravelings found while you are ironing can be snipped right then and there.

❀

When ironing, prevent clothes from slipping off the ironing board by keeping them on with straight pins. This idea is especially helpful with items having many pleats and tucks, and with large pieces like tablecloths and sheets, whose weight is likely to pull them toward the floor.

❀

When ironing linen napkins or handkerchiefs, separate the everyday ones from those saved for a special occasion by folding the worn ones in squares and the especially nice ones in triangles.

❀

Try ironing in the bedroom: Closet hangers are near at hand and the bed is an ideal place to sort things in separate piles.

❀

Tackle weekly ironing with a neighbor who hates the task, too: Set aside a given time each week and bring clothes, iron and board to one another's home, alternating weeks. Iron each other's clothes, or pool them together and work from one basket.

❀

After washing your ironing board cover, put it back on the board while still damp. The surface will be completely smooth when the cover is dry.

❀

When holes appear in an ironing board cover, mend them with iron-on patches.

❀

If your family prefers cloth napkins to paper ones, avoid long hours of ironing by substituting high-quality, closely woven dishcloths in solid pastels. Especially nice for youngsters because of their softness, dishcloth napkins look just as pretty rolled up in napkin rings as do the regular variety.

Windows, Walls, Curtains and Upholstery

When washing windows, clean dirt out of the corners by covering the eraser end of the pencil with a cleaning rag and forcing it into the crevices.

❀

Instead of covering a broom in cheesecloth to dust moldings and upper walls, make a permanent, washable broom cover from a discarded shirt sleeve. Cut the sleeve off at the elbow; stitch the raw ends together. Slip the sleeve over the broom and button the cuff around the handle.

❀

When washing woodwork, save walls from soiling by holding a piece of cardboard along the edge of the woodwork as you wash.

❀

Put cotton gloves or socks on your hands to wipe Venetian blinds clean. The process is faster using your hands, as it is easier to get at hard-to-reach areas.

❀

Instead of removing long draperies when working on floors or shampooing carpets, hang a wire coat hanger on the drapery rods and lift the bottoms of the draperies onto them. The drapes will stay clean and will not wrinkle.

❀

When Venetian-blind tapes look faded and worn—especially when new curtains have been added to windows—use a small amount of the material from the curtains to "replace" the tapes. Cut strips about two inches wider than the tapes. Hem the raw edges and sew the strips to the tape along the top edge, folding each side under the tape. Use a large tacking stitch to hem one side of the material to the other (not sewing it to the tape except at the top and bottom).

❀

When the white tapes on Venetian blinds become soiled, brighten by rubbing on white liquid shoe polish.

❀

In a room where sunlight strikes with more force at some windows than others, rotate the curtains each time they are cleaned. For easy identification, mark each pair with a bit of colored yarn or cloth sewn into the hems on the wrong side.

❀

Child-proof a sofa by covering the cushion bottoms with vinyl. Turn the cushions right side up when company comes.

❀

After washing slipcovers, ease the dreaded job of tugging and pulling covers back onto the furniture by wearing a pair of kid gloves. The job will be less aggravating and fingernails will remain unbroken.

❀

Cover the upholstered seat of a dining room chair that is used by a small child with half a yard of clear plastic. Spilled food is quickly whisked off with a damp cloth; the fabric underneath is kept clean and unharmed.

Spots, Stains and Odors

To take fruit stains out of material, stretch fabric over the mouth of a glass canning jar. Gently screw the ring section of the cap over the material to hold it in place. Then pour boiling water over the stain.

❀

Use a small, cheap paintbrush to brush detergent onto spots and stains before washing: It helps economize with laundry soap and keeps hands in better condition.

❀

Use undiluted ammonia to remove bath-oil rings from bathtubs.

❀

Oil-based paints can be removed from the skin with plain baby oil.

❀

Ballpoint ink can be removed from skin with margarine and a damp cloth.

❀

To remove ballpoint ink from material, dab on concentrated hair shampoo or spray on hair spray, rub the ink out, then launder the item as usual.

❀

Four parts turpentine to one part linseed oil, applied with a soft cloth, removes spots, cleans and shines wooden furniture.

❀

Foam shaving cream removes spots from rugs.

❀

Shampoo is an effective grease remover and is not abrasive. It can be used on a wide variety of things— from a baby's skin to bathroom utilities.

❀

Rub lemon juice on hands to remove vegetable stains or the smell of onions, garlic or fish.

❀

If your garbage disposer has a bad odor, grind up lemon slices in it; the odor will disappear.

❀

After cleaning an oven, eliminate the unpleasant odor by "baking" orange peelings briefly at 350°.

❀

To give the whole house a delicate, exotic odor while humidifying the air, place a pan of water on radiators or heaters and drop in a few empty pods of cardamom.

❀

Give dresser drawers, linen closets, wardrobes and clothes closets a nice, fresh scent by putting open, empty bottles of perfume or stick cologne in them.

❈

Fill old stockings with mothballs, cloves, or pine needles and tie over the rods in closets.

❈

A small sachet placed under the ironing board cover will give a nice fragrance to freshly ironed clothes.

❈

Lighted candles will keep rooms clear of cigarette smoke, even during parties. Candles can also be used to clear smoke out of the kitchen if something burns or runs over in the oven.

Clean-up Catchall

Polish brass doorknobs without removing the entire lock from the door by making a shield to protect the woodwork. Cut a hole, the size of the fixture flange, in a piece of cardboard; tape the shield securely in place.

❈

Protect floors when moving heavy furniture by slipping an old sock or mitten over each leg.

❈

When loop bedroom rugs become soft and wrinkled, treat them as follows: Wash and dry the usual way, then turn the rug over and, using a dish mop, pat thick, cooked starch all over the back. Dry again. The rugs stay stiff and wrinkle-free until the next washing.

❀

Lessen damage to furniture during a move by taping legs, edges, and metalwork with masking tape. To remove tape, pull off slowly.

❀

Spray furniture polish over hard-to-clean ashtrays, such as those made of silver or pewter. The ashes dump out without sticking and leave no odor or ash. Reapply wax when necessary.

❀

Slip an old pair of socks over your hands when rubbing off metal polish; silver or brass surfaces will glow radiantly.

❀

Use an old shaving brush to clean pleated lampshades: The bristles are long enough to remove dust easily from the folds but soft enough not to injure the fabric.

❀

Clean shower curtain hooks by putting them in a sock and knotting it, then washing them with your next load of clothes.

❀

When washing squeaky toys, put adhesive over the opening; no water will squeeze out after the cleaning.

❊

Glue from store labels that remains on glassware can be removed by dabbing the area with transparent tape.

❊

Use fingernail polish remover to take off lingering bits of adhesive tape. First be sure the surface is solvent-resistant.

❊

To remove mineral deposits from a shower head, place the head in a pan and cover with vinegar. Simmer fifteen to twenty minutes; rinse with cold water.

❊

To remove old stickers and decals from metallic surfaces, place a heat lamp over the decal for five to ten minutes.

❊

Car upholstery can be protected from greasy work clothes by covering the seats with fitted bed sheets. The sheets can be removed easily for family travel and replaced quickly after washing.

❊

To prevent birds from roosting in branches over a parked car, spray water into the tree each evening. The birds, with a few obstinate exceptions, will soon get the message; the car will stay cleaner.

2.

Home Organization and Storage

Clothes and Accessories

Use old nightgowns or robes to "slipcover" good suits and dresses before summer or winter storage.

❀

Out-of-season clothes will stay dry even in damp basements if stored in lidded plastic trash cans.

❀

Free drawer space by storing bulky sweaters in a purse file that hangs in the closet.

❀

Attach a padded towel rod to the inside of a closet door for hanging slacks; they will stay nice and smooth.

❀

Instead of spending money on expensive clothing hangers: Cut a thin cellulose sponge in small strips and attach them to the ends of wire trouser hangers with china cement.

❀

Keep pantyhose and stockings snag-free by storing them in plastic sandwich bags.

❀

Make a clothes hanger for a nursery without a closet. Take a long, heavy-duty cardboard cylinder and cover it with felt or flannel. Cover an aluminum pie pan with the same material, invert it, and dangle cutouts from the rim. Place the decorated pan on top of the roll and fit it securely to the ceiling. Insert cup hooks around the roll.

❀

Sort outgrown clothes that are to be handed down in the family by placing them in separate boxes according to the year, season and size of clothes, and label the boxes with the appropriate information. In this way you will not have to rely on memory and will not overlook items.

❀

Store young children's tiny socks in pressed-paper egg cartons. Paint the individual egg cups to match the socks.

❀

When children must share a closet, prevent arguments over space by painting each half a different color. Paint clothes hangers to match each child's side.

❀

Provide each child in the family with a cardboard box (which can be painted or covered with contact paper to match room decor) to use as a clothes hamper. Give the children the responsibility of carrying their boxes of soiled clothes to the washing area on wash days. Clothes can be folded and sorted right from the dryer into each box and the children can return them to their rooms.

❀

Attach an accordion clothes hanger to the wall in the room where you dress and hang accessories— necklaces, scarves, belts, hats—from it. This not only frees dresser drawer space, but adds a decorative touch to the room.

❀

An extra shelf for hats can be made by tying rows of cord between screw eyes above a closet's top shelf.

❀

Decorate round oatmeal or cornmeal boxes and use as closet hat stands. Store inside them the gloves, scarf or special accessories you wear with each particular hat.

❀

Attach a multi-skirt hanger or shoe bag to the closet door for hanging gloves, hats and scarves.

❀

Build a wooden trough inside closet doors; attach a line of cup hooks to the bottom of the trough. Hang belts, hats, scarves from the hooks; put in the trough your combs, brushes, keys, sunglasses and other items that have a habit of getting lost.

❀

Make a belt holder by removing the metal spine from a three-ring notebook binder and attaching it horizontally with screws to the inside of the closet door.

❀

To make a tie rack, glue felt to curtain rods and attach the rods inside the closet door.

❀

Those who love jewelry but do not like to put it away may prefer to use a stuffed animal as an alternative to a jewelry box. Put the animal on the dressing table; hang necklaces around its neck and pin other jewelry on.

❀

Keep fine chains from tangling in the jewelry box by cutting a drinking straw to half the length of the chain, slipping the chain through and fastening the catch.

In the Kitchen

Where space for linens is limited, hang place mats and tablecloths from a multi-skirt hanger on the back of the kitchen door.

❀

Where shelf space is limited, roll towels, aprons, and other linens. More than twice the number of items can be stored in the same space.

❀

Put unopened staples, such as sugar, puddings and flour, upside down on the shelf; in this way one can tell at a glance if it is time to purchase new reserves.

❀

Make an organization center in the kitchen. Hang a bulletin board on the wall; cut paper plates in half  and thumbtack them to the board to form pockets; label each pocket for such things as "pens and pencils," "stamps," "letters to be mailed," "letters to be answered," "bills." Also tack a calendar and a tablet of paper to the bulletin board.

❀

Put a revolving tie rack near the kitchen sink, for holding brushes, measuring spoons and other small utensils.

❀

Keep a glass jar in a kitchen drawer: When anyone finds a small item—a button, screw, tack, bead —and does not know where it belongs, put it in the jar. Anyone who misses such an item will have a place to start looking.

❀

Use stackable wire baskets to store many kitchen items. Their openness allows air to circulate freely around vegetables such as potatoes or onions, which rot quickly in closed bins; damp items, such as brushes, sponges, and cleaning rags, can dry quickly.

❀

A 24-bottle soda case hung on the wall in the kitchen or sewing room makes good pigeonhole storage for small items.

❀

Make a lazy Susan inside a kitchen cupboard for easy access to small bottles or spice tins. Punch a hole in the bottom of an aluminum pie pan. Loosely screw the pan to the cupboard shelf—the pan will twirl easily.

❀

To store a rolling pin conveniently, screw two wire coat hooks on the inside of a cupboard, just far enough apart to slip each handle of the rolling pin over the lower curve of the hook.

❀

For easy access to electrical appliance cords, hang cords over brightly colored spools which have been nailed to spare kitchen wall space.

In a Child's Room

Make a rack for storing children's odds and ends by gluing several 46-ounce cans together with the open ends facing the same way. Spray paint. Set the rack on its side, like a wine rack: Into it can go comic books, art supplies, small toys and the paraphernalia children collect.

❀

Rather than buy two desks for two preteens who share a room, use a dinette table and four chairs. The surface is large enough for both to work simultaneously and it doubles as a game table when friends visit. Decorate several coffee or juice cans with adhesive paper and place them on a small plastic lazy

Susan to hold supplies. Paper and large items can be stored in a dresser drawer.

❀

Put casters on a drawer from a discarded dresser to make a toy or storage bin that can be rolled under the bed.

❀

Stackable plastic vegetable bins are attractive, inexpensive and easy to clean when used to store children's toys. If children share a bedroom, let each have his own color bins.

❀

Make a decorative "cage" for children's stuffed toys: Fold a fishnet in half and attach it to the bedroom wall with thumbtacks or nails; put animals between folds.

❀

To display children's artwork without ruining walls with tape or tacks, hang fishnet over one wall. Hold pictures to the net with clothespins. Bulky items, such as cowboy hats, can be pinned to the net as well.

❀

Make a storage cabinet for a child by gluing kitchen matchboxes together. Cover the outside with contact paper. Use a two-pronged paper fastener as a handle on each drawer. A rope handle can be stapled to the top.

❀

To provide space for extra baby blankets and towels, attach curtain rods to the back of the headboard of a baby's crib.

❋

A brightly colored plywood board placed across the lower rungs of a highchair makes a convenient shelf on which to keep a box of small toys, a bib, a box of tissues, etc.

❋

Keep a gaily painted half-bushel basket under a baby's bath table to hold soiled clothes. Line the basket with plastic cloth which has been trimmed with pink or blue bias tape.

. . . and All Around the House

Instead of a filing cabinet, use a hanging plastic purse file to store papers, letters and receipts. Each clear plastic pouch will hold six to ten standard file folders. The file can be hung in a closet near your desk.

❋

Make a desk caddy from half-gallon milk cartons. Group cartons together and draw a slanted line down both sides. Cut cartons along lines and across the back and front. "Glue" the cartons together by covering them—and taping the rims—with colorful contact paper.

❋

Add narrow plywood partitions lengthwise to deep drawers. Put most-used articles on the half-shelves.

❀

Hanging a mirror in the back of a deep linen closet helps keep track of stored items.

❀

Store winter bedding in the large plastic or paper bags from the dry cleaner. Slip one folded blanket or quilt into each bag, add moth crystals, fold the end of the bag over and seal with transparent tape.

❀

To catch the overflow from the bathroom's medicine chest, attach spice racks inside the linen-closet door. The racks are the right size for bottles and packages, and items can be spotted immediately.

❀

Make a "clearance corner" in your house or apartment by putting a cardboard box in an unused niche. Each time you find something you know will never be used again, put it in the box. This not only frees storage space for necessary items, but eliminates time wasted in hunting for articles to donate to charity.

❀

An old chest placed in the hallway near the front door serves as a storage space for rubbers and boots —as well as a convenient place to sit while putting them on.

❀

Set up a large carton in the garage or basement to store "trash"—old jars, newspapers, mailing tubes, yarn, cloth scraps, broken jewelry, old candles, bleach bottles, egg cartons, etc.—and donate these "found objects" to the local school art teacher, whose supply is often limited.

❀

Keep an easy inventory of boxed closet storage, without having to climb on a chair or ladder. Attach a tag identifying the boxes' contents to a long cord. The cord should hang down far enough so that it can be easily read.

❀

For people who cannot throw paperbacks away: Keep a shelf behind the front door for books which will probably not be read again. When visitors arrive, ask if there is anything on the shelf they would like to have.

❀

Provide a box in some part of the house in which family members can drop memorabilia—notes, photos, invitations, ticket stubs. At the end of each year, make a family album out of the collected material.

❀

Make an appliance notebook using a three-ring binder, with divider pages marked "Washer," "Freezer," "TV," etc. In each section, keep all instruction booklets, guarantees, receipts pertaining to the appliance—just punch holes in the papers and slip them onto the rings.

❀

Using bright yellow paint, mark regular parking stalls in the garage for children's bicycles and wagons.

Draw an outline of the vehicle that belongs in each stall. With identifiable places, children will "park" their vehicles in the same way in which they see their parents parking the family car.

❀

To avoid searching for photo negatives, store them behind corresponding prints in your photograph album.

❀

Carry an open-ended eyeglass case in your purse to store pens, pencils, fingernail files, small scissors, etc.

❀

Turn an old glove into a belt holder for small items such as pens, tools, golf tees. Fold cuff over on itself and stitch down to form a loop that will slide over a belt. Slit glove fingers where they meet the palm; hand stitch raw edges to strengthen.

❀

Keep all beauty creams and lotions in a dresser drawer that has been lined with oilcloth; any marks left by the cosmetics can be washed off in seconds.

3.

Kitchen Hints

General, Storage and Shopping

Make a kitchen notebook, listing unusual ingredients not normally kept on hand—one ingredient to a page. Whenever you find a new recipe with such an ingredient, write the name of the recipe on that page. Then, for example, if you have made a recipe which requires some buttermilk, you can refer to the buttermilk page for other recipes to use up the remaining buttermilk.

❀

Cover a shorthand notebook with contact paper and fill it with recipes; the book stands up easily for reference while cooking. Sponge off the cover when necessary.

❀

To hold a cookbook propped open, make a holder from a wire clothes hanger. Bend hanger as shown in diagram. The holder can be decorated by twining yarn around the hanger and adding tassels.

❀

For convenience when cooking and baking, glue a cork to the top of a recipe file box, cut a slit in it and set the recipe card in the slit when in use.

❀

To keep recipe cards clean and conveniently in view while cooking, hang a paper clamp from a thumbtack inside the cupboard door just over the work counter. Open the door and clip the recipe card to the clamp for easy reference as you cook.

❀

Before big company dinners, write out a menu and tape it to the outside of a kitchen cabinet door. Refer to the list when placing food on the table. That way, no dishes will be forgotten.

❀

Keep a notebook, divided into sections of about four pages for each month in the year, to record highly praised menus that feature seasonal produce and fruits.

❀

When packaging food for the freezer, write the expiration date of the contents on the label, rather than the date on which the item was stored. This method makes it easier to avoid waste.

❀

Keep heavy oven mitts near the freezer to wear when you hunt for items.

❀

Use white shelf paper to line the back and ends of the basement cupboard where home-canned foods are stored. The paper virtually acts like a lightbulb; it is easy to find what is needed at a glance.

❀

If the garbage pickup is several days away, place quick-to-spoil kitchen refuse, such as fish heads or chicken bones, in a bag marked "garbage" and freeze immediately. Put it out on garbage day.

❀

To save room in lunch boxes, use empty pillboxes with snap-on tops for items such as sugar, salt and pepper.

❀

If space for ice cube trays is limited, use plastic egg cartons—they can be cut down to size.

❀

When shortening cans are empty, store without washing. These already-greased tins make excellent containers for storing refrigerator-roll dough; the tight lids allow no air to form a crust and the tins take up less refrigerator space than bowls.

❀

When extra ice cubes are needed for a party, use muffin tins instead of buying extra ice cube trays. The pans make big ice cubes that last longer.

❀

When making sandwiches, only one trip to the refrigerator will be necessary if you store all sandwich makings—such as mayonnaise, mustard, catsup, luncheon meat, cheese, pickles, etc.—on a tray in the refrigerator.

❀

To allow more cabinet space for canned goods, keep an extra bread box in the kitchen just for the baby's special foods.

❀

On hot summer days, take an insulated beach bag to the supermarket; put frozen items in the bag for the trip home.

❀

To keep grocery bags upright in the back of a station wagon, fit a spring-tension curtain rod across the back compartment to make a pen for the packages.

❀

Write shopping lists on envelopes so that you have a place to tuck coupons, trading stamps or receipts.

❀

To remind you to turn off the stove before going on errands, put a potholder on top of your pocketbook.

❀

If you enjoy company while preparing meals, put a rocking chair in an unused corner of the kitchen—it will give an instant, inviting country kitchen atmosphere.

Dishwashing and Defrosting

Where everyone eats on a different schedule, dishwashing can be eliminated in busy households by leaving the sink filled with sudsy water: After finishing a meal, each person washes his or her own dishes and puts them in the drainer to dry.

❀

When scouring, hold steel wool in a sponge. The sponge protects the hands and absorbs water, so that the job is less messy.

❋

To remove mineral rings inside glass coffeepots, fill with three parts vinegar to one part water; let stand until rings dissolve.

❋

Burned pots and pans can be cleaned by filling with boiling water and either a few crystals of citric acid (sour salt) or a few tablespoons of vinegar, and heating for an hour or two.

❋

When defrosting the refrigerator, use a siphon to eliminate the messy task of emptying the tray under the freezer compartment. Simply shut off the refrigerator and siphon off the water as it collects.

❋

When defrosting a refrigerator, clean the crisper pan first, put the ice trays and frozen foods in it, and close. Foods will stay frozen while the refrigerator is being cleaned.

❋

To defrost the refrigerator quickly, put a pot of boiling water in the freezer compartment while you wash the rest of the interior. By the time you have finished, built-up ice will have loosened in chunks; finish the job with a few blasts of hot air from your hairdryer.

❋

Slit a small pocket in a sponge and insert all pieces of soap that are not used up. The sudsy sponge can be used for bathing, cleaning pots and pans, scrubbing sinks, etc.

Kitchen Catchall: Cooking Techniques and Food Ideas

Turn a metal colander upside down over the skillet when frying food. This allows steam to escape, but keeps the fat from spattering.

❀

Put marbles in the bottom of the double boiler. When the water boils down, the marbles will make enough racket to call you from the farthest corner of the house.

❀

Drop a thimble over the center tube in a percolator coffeepot before adding ground coffee; filling the pot will be easier without having to worry about grounds falling into the water.

❀

Prevent a crust from forming inside the lids and edges of jars of mustard, chili sauce, pickles, olives, honey, etc., by putting a piece of plastic wrap over the top of the jar before screwing the lid on.

❀

Push a straw to the bottom of a new bottle of catsup—the catsup will flow faster.

❁

A powder puff kept in the flour canister comes in handy when you are dusting flour on a rolling pin or pastry board.

❁

Use fresh herbs all year around: When homegrown mint, parsley, basil, chives, etc., are ready, chop them in a blender with a little water. Spoon the minced leaves into foil-lined egg cartons and freeze. Place individually wrapped foil portions in a plastic bag and store for use throughout the winter. Freshly thawed, the herbs are much tastier than dried versions.

❁

A garlic press can be used for many jobs: to pulverize hard-boiled-egg yolks for garnishing salads or to make smooth stuffing for deviled eggs; to puree small amounts of food for a baby; to mash a few vegetables for soup; to pulverize foods too small to put in a blender.

❁

The quickest way to heat a baby bottle is to place it in a tall, narrow tin can filled to the brim with water. The thin metal allows the water to heat rapidly; because the entire bottle is submerged, the milk heats quickly and evenly.

❁

Use wooden or plastic toothpicks to raise paraffin wax from jelly jars, or to clean the crevices in fine china or glass.

❀

Wash paraffin removed from opened jelly jars and store it in a pint jar. When jelly-making time arrives, put the jar in water on the stove to melt wax, adding new paraffin if needed. This eliminates cleaning wax from a pot. After using, cool and cover any remaining wax for future use.

❀

Use a gravy boat when filling jars or jelly tumblers: The boat can be readily dipped into hot liquid by the handle, and the long spout fits almost any size opening, preventing spilling and waste of the liquid.

❀

Tape or glue canning labels to the nonreusable lids instead of to the sides of the jars—no more struggling to remove labels when the contents are gone.

❀

To keep molasses, corn syrup or honey from sticking to a spoon or measuring cup, rinse utensil with hot water before using.

❀

In summer months, insulated aluminum-foil ice cream bags can be used as lunch carriers. Pack the lunch the night before and put it in the bag, in the freezer. The next morning, take the bag out when you leave the house and keep it in a desk drawer when you arrive at work. By lunchtime, it will have thawed to exactly the right temperature for cool summer eating.

※

To remove fat from hot soup, put an ice cube in a thin cloth and swish back and forth in soup; the fat will collect on the cloth.

※

To make extra-creamy split-pea soup, beat with a rotary beater for a few minutes just before serving. It will not be necessary to strain or thicken the soup.

※

When soup or stock recipes call for a bouquet garni, save time and trouble by putting the spices in a tea ball instead of making a cheesecloth bag.

※

After making soup in quantity, fill bread pans or ice trays with it and freeze. When frozen, turn soup out of trays and put in plastic bags. The soup will take up less space in the freezer when stored in this manner.

※

To degrease without effort, put a piece of waxed paper directly on top of stews, stocks and soups before refrigerating. When the liquid has cooled, peel the paper off; the fat will come off with it.

※

To crack a quantity of nuts quickly, put them into a bag and gently hammer until all are broken open. Then pour them into a bowl and pick out the meat.

※

To get Brazil nuts out of the shells unbroken, freeze them until the shells crack.

❃

For those allergic to nuts—Chinese noodles make a good substitute to use in recipes.

❃

To provide a creamier taste to such items as pumpkin pie, instant potatoes, pancake batter, etc., add 2 or 3 tablespoons of powdered creamer.

❃

Make "instant white sauce" cubes. Blend 1 cup soft butter with 1 cup flour. Spread in an ice cube tray; chill well; cut into 16 cubes; and store in a plastic bag in the freezer. For a medium-thick sauce, drop 1 cube in 1 cup of cold milk and heat, stirring as it thickens.

❃

When a cream sauce does not thicken to the proper consistency, add a tablespoon or more of crushed, ready-to-eat dry cereal just before serving. It does not alter the flavor and is fail-proof.

❃

For thickening gravy, sauce or stew, sprinkle instant mashed potatoes into the mixture and stir. It's quick and simple: Lumps dissolve immediately.

❃

When low on condiments, mix together a little mayonnaise, mustard, catsup, leftover relish or chopped sweet pickles and chopped onions. It makes a good relish that will adequately serve the whole family.

❀

Save small amounts of jams and jellies in one jar; heat to make a thick syrup for pancakes.

❀

Before throwing away jam and jelly containers, fill with hot water and shake. Use the sweetened water when making gelatin desserts.

❀

Freeze syrup from canned fruit to make a sauce for gingerbread, coffee cake or nut bread. To 2 cups syrup, add 1 tablespoon butter and 1 tablespoon lemon juice; heat until bubbly. Thicken with 2 tablespoons flour.

❀

Make fruit-flavored syrup for pancakes and waffles by combining 1 cup of any fruit juice with 2 cups of sugar and cooking the mixture until it boils.

❀

For a new flavor, toast cheese sandwiches in a frying pan lightly greased with bacon fat.

❀

Give a Middle Eastern flavor to after-dinner coffee by adding a crushed pod of cardamom to the pot.

Meats, Poultry and Fish

General

Put flour and seasonings in a salt shaker when flouring meats, poultry or fish. This prevents waste and is less messy than rolling the meat in flour.

❀

Save small bits of cornflakes, crackers and bread crumbs in a closed glass jar. Add a little flour and use the crumbs to bread chops, meat patties or fish cakes.

❀

Vinegar is a natural meat tenderizer.

❀

Crushed pretzels are a good substitute for bread crumbs in meat loaf.

❀

Stretch hash by adding ground-up apples.

❀

Add crushed corn bread or cornflakes, instead of bread crumbs, to meatballs.

❀

Add onion-flavored potato chip crumbs to meatballs.

❀

Grind luncheon meat and add to 3 cups of white sauce. Season with salt and pepper, onion salt and parsley. Serve over mashed potatoes, rice, noodles, waffles, toast or pancakes.

❀

Collect leftover green beans, peas, corn, potatoes, onions and celery in a plastic container in the freezer. Add the vegetable mix to beef stew.

❀

Pour about half a cup of sweet pickle juice over beef, ham or pork before roasting.

❀

Roast lamb in a blanket of leftover garlic bread. Attach bread, buttered side next to meat, with toothpicks; sprinkle with water; roast. The garlic butter flavors the meat; the bread makes a dressing.

❀

Grind cooked lamb, raw carrots and onions; season and spread on biscuit dough rolled out in a rectangle. Roll up, jelly roll style, and bake. Serve hot. (Can be served with a mushroom sauce.)

❀

Fasten sausages together on a meat skewer before frying—one flip with a spatula turns them all. This also cuts down on spattering.

❀

Use pliers to peel the skin from a boiled tongue.

❀

Before opening a package of bacon, roll it into a tube. This loosens the slices, keeping them from sticking together.

❀

Crumble extra bacon and use it as a topping for salads or casseroles.

❀

Add crumbled, cold bacon to cream sauces for vegetables.

❀

Use bacon fat for popping corn; drain on brown paper; add salt.

❀

Boil wieners in bread-and-butter-pickle juice and a small amount of water.

❀

When going on a picnic, put hot dogs in a wide-mouthed thermos and fill with boiling water. The franks will be ready to eat by the time the picnic spot is reached.

Poultry

Chicken, rolled in powdered milk instead of flour, will fry to a golden brown.

❀

If hot fried chicken is not to be eaten immediately, cover it with aluminum foil and punch holes in the

foil. The holes will allow steam to escape; the crust
will not become soggy.

❀

When grilling poultry, use dental floss for tying the
bird to the grill and for trussing. Dental floss does not
burn and is very strong.

❀

Use a curved upholstery needle when trussing a
fowl.

❀

Make chicken dressing with the chicken. Crumble
stale breads—corn bread, biscuits, crackers and loaf
bread—into a mixing bowl. Heat a can of chicken
broth; pour over bread and cover; let steam while
chopping parsley, celery and onions. Season vegetables
with poultry seasoning, salt and pepper, an unbeaten
egg, 1 tablespoon butter. Mix with softened bread;
bake until golden in a glass pie plate.

❀

To prevent leftover poultry stuffing from being too
dry, add 1 egg and ½ to 1 cup of milk before baking
a second time.

❀

Save and freeze bits of chicken and vegetables such
as carrots, celery, potatoes and onions to make a
chicken pie. When ready to use, thaw and cube the
chicken; heat vegetables in a little butter, add a package of dehydrated chicken-noodle mix and blend,
adding a little milk and the chicken. Thicken broth
with cornstarch or flour; place all ingredients in a

baking dish; cover with a crust and bake. For extra flavor, add celery seed to the crust.

❀

Give leftover turkey an Oriental touch: Drain a can of water chestnuts; slice; lightly brown in butter. Add a can of turkey gravy, a dash of soy or Worcestershire sauce, and the turkey. Serve over toast or noodles.

Fish

Bake fish on a bed of chopped onion, celery and parsley. This adds a nice flavor and keeps fish from sticking to the pan.

❀

Instead of using kitchen counter tops and cutting boards for cleaning fish and game, make a portable work table by covering an old ironing board with linoleum. The board can be used outside; it is adjustable and easily cleaned and stored.

❀

Banish the odor of fish from cooking and serving utensils by rinsing in vinegar water.

❀

Stretch tuna fish salad by adding diced or grated apples and celery.

❀

Put leftover scrambled eggs in tuna or chicken salads.

Potatoes, Rice, Breads and Grain

When making mashed potatoes, save some of the water in which they were boiled; mix with powdered milk and add the liquid to the potatoes when mashing. This restores many nutrients lost in the cooking.

❀

Use sour cream, instead of milk, in mashed potatoes.

❀

When mashing potatoes with no butter on hand, add several tablespoons of cream cheese.

❀

Put leftover mashed potatoes in a well-buttered cake pan; sprinkle lightly with paprika and grated cheese; dot with butter. Bake ½ hour until brown and puffy.

❀

Sprinkle cinnamon over raw potatoes before frying.

❀

When grating potatoes for pancakes, add a little sour cream; this will keep potatoes from discoloring.

❀

Add a dash of nutmeg to potato salad.

❀

To stretch leftover potato salad, serve in green peppers that have been boiled 5 minutes in salted water, drained and brushed with barbecue sauce. Serve cold.

❀

Drain leftover potato salad and fry in 1 tablespoon butter until brown.

❀

After buying a large-quantity bag of potatoes, sort them out according to size, and place each in its own categorized storage area: the medium size for baking; the largest for cutting up in chowders, stews and casserole dishes; the smallest ones for boiling in their jackets.

❀

Make rice fluffier and whiter by adding 1 teaspoon lemon juice to each quart of water.

❀

Cook a small amount of leftover hamburger meat with the onions when making Spanish rice.

❀

To add flavor and nutrition to hominy grits or rice, cook them in liquid saved from cooking vegetables or drained from canned vegetables. Wheat germ added to the grits or rice also adds nutrition and a nice nutty taste.

❀

To avoid overboiling or the necessity of stirring when you cook thin noodles, simply bring the required amount of water to a boil, add noodles, turn off heat, cover and let stand for twenty minutes. Drain as usual. The noodles will turn out perfectly cooked every time and they won't stick to the pan.

❀

Make a better French toast batter by using sour milk with a little soda in place of sweet milk.

❀

Nutmeg toast is a nice change from cinnamon toast.

❀

Save toast for making croutons for soup or salads. Cut toast into cubes and use as is, or fry in garlic butter.

❀

Turn leftover hot dog buns into bread sticks by cutting buns in half lengthwise, then cutting each piece into three sticks. Butter and sprinkle with cheese. Put in the broiler and toast on all sides.

❀

Rejuvenate stale, hard loaves of Italian or French bread by holding the bread under running water for a few seconds, then wrapping it in foil and placing it in a 150°-200° F. oven for 15 minutes. It will come out as soft as fresh-baked bread. For a crunchy crust, remove the bread from the oven after 15 minutes; uncover; baste the loaves with butter and return them to the oven for 5 to 10 minutes.

❀

Make a dessert from stale French or Italian bread by cutting the bread into ½" slices and covering them with warm milk that has been boiled with lemon peel and sugar to taste. When bread is thoroughly soaked, drain well; dip in beaten egg; fry in small amount of hot oil until both sides are brown. Roll in sugar and cinnamon, or dribble honey over bread. Eat hot.

❀

Save bread heels to make pudding. Tear 10 heels, plus 6 to 7 extra slices, in bite-size pieces; put in a shallow, greased 2-quart baking dish. Sprinkle with 1 cup raisins. Beat 3 eggs with ½ cup sugar until thickened. Scald 1 quart milk. Pour a small amount of scalded milk into the eggs; stir. Then stir egg-milk mixture into the rest of the milk; add 1 teaspoon vanilla. Pour over bread in baking dish; make certain all bread is moistened. Sprinkle with cinnamon; bake for 30 minutes in a 325° F. oven. Serve warm or cold with cream; makes 8 servings.

❀

Dark raisin bread is a delicious filler to use in apple brown Betty.

❀

Freeze leftover waffles; when ready to use them, reheat them in a toaster.

❀

Chop or grate fruit into leftover waffle batter; drop mixture by spoonfuls into ½″ hot bacon fat; fry until golden. Roll fritters in powdered sugar.

❀

Cook a batch of waffles ahead of time and keep them in a low-temperature oven before brunch guests arrive.

❀

Make pancakes without milk. Substitute club soda or ginger ale. Reduce the amount of sugar when making the batter with ginger ale.

❀

Put cooked cereal into empty juice cans and refrigerate. When ready to use, cut into ½″ slices; fry. Serve with butter and syrup.

❀

Give breakfast oatmeal a raisin-spice flavor: Combine 1 teaspoon cinnamon, ¼ teaspoon nutmeg and ½ cup raisins. Stir spices and raisins into boiling salted water just before adding oatmeal. Add oatmeal and cook as usual. Delicious served with cream and sugar.

❀

Potato chip crumbs make great casserole toppings; added to salads at the last minute, they give a nice crunch.

Eggs, Butter and Cheese

Before hard-boiling eggs, pierce the rounded end with a needle: The shells will not crack while cooking and peeling will be easier.

❀

Keep separated egg yolks up to three weeks using this method: Place them gently in a pan of cold water; cook over medium heat 5 minutes or until desired hardness; freeze. The taste is not affected, and the yolks can be used later for such things as potato salad or anything requiring hard-boiled eggs.

❧

To separate the egg white from the yolk, break the egg over a small funnel. The white will glide through, the yolk will remain.

❧

Make a Western omelet when the refrigerator is bare: Chop leftover bits of ham, green pepper, celery, parsley; if eggs need stretching, add a little milk and bread crumbs.

❧

Bring eggs to room temperature quickly by placing them in a bowl with very warm tap water. Cover for 3 to 5 minutes.

❧

When a recipe calls for softened butter, but you have forgotten to take it out of the refrigerator in advance, measure the correct amount and shred it as you would a carrot. The small pieces will be soft enough to work with immediately.

❧

Save money and calories by whipping your own butter: Use one pound butter, in bulk, and one pound margarine. Whip in a mixer or by hand and store in covered refrigerator dishes.

❋

Use an ice cream scoop to measure solid shortening. Dip it into the shortening can, use the metal rim to level off the shortening and empty it into your measuring cup.

❋

For the diet-conscious: Make imitation sour cream by whirling creamed cottage cheese in a blender. It can be flavored with sugar, extracts, chives, etc., or used in place of mayonnaise in coleslaw or potato and macaroni salads.

❋

For those who like greens or fruits garnished with blue or Roquefort cheese: Keep bulk packages of cheese in the freezer; when needed, scrape the edge of the cheese with a paring knife. It will crumble beautifully and be ready to eat by the time the dressing is added.

Vegetables and Salads

Vegetables

Only half as much butter is needed for seasoning vegetables if butter is browned before it is added. The browning brings out the butter's flavor.

❋

Save the water used when shredding vegetables in the blender. The water is full of nutrients and adds flavor to soups, stocks and stews.

❀

Puree leftover vegetables and use to enrich canned soups or consommés.

❀

Pour Italian or French dressing over leftover green beans right after dinner while they are still warm. Marinate in the refrigerator for at least a day; serve cold over slices of tomato and onions; garnish with rings of black olives.

❀

Stretch green beans with chopped onions and celery.

❀

Fry leftover kidney beans in bacon fat. Add water if consistency is too thick.

❀

Add salt after cooking dried beans; putting the salt in at the beginning hardens the beans and slows the cooking.

❀

Grate cooked beets, mix them with horseradish and add to applesauce. Serve with roast pork.

❀

Blend peas or chopped broccoli with grated Cheddar cheese and mayonnaise; stuff into celery; serve cold.

❀

Make cooked carrots more palatable for the whole family by adding a little horseradish and sugar.

❀

Dill-pickle juice is a good marinade for carrot sticks.

❀

Season creamed or whole-kernel corn with curry powder or a pinch of marjoram, thyme or savory.

❀

Make a board for cutting sweet corn off the cob by pounding a three-inch nail into a one-foot-square board. Push the corn, stem-end down, onto the nail. The corn will turn easily on the nail as you cut.

❀

Add whole-kernel corn to hamburger relish for a quick corn relish; keep refrigerated.

❀

Marinate hot cooked corn in Italian or French dressing; stuff into small, whole tomatoes; serve cold.

❀

Stretch cooked corn or succotash with chopped olives.

❀

When making pickles, clean and smooth cucumbers with a nylon net scrubber ball.

❀

To keep eggplant shells intact for use in stuffed eggplant, scoop the pulp out with a grapefruit knife *before* parboiling. Parboil shells and pulp at the same time.

❀

To prevent garlic bulbs from drying out, peel each clove and put in a covered jar of vegetable oil. The garlic will remain fresh; the oil's flavor will be enhanced for salad dressings.

❀

Fresh garlic keeps indefinitely in the freezer. Section the garlic head into cloves and place them in a small freezer container. When you are ready to use some, take out a clove, peel it and use without thawing.

❀

Sauté mushrooms with a dash of marjoram.

❀

Avoid tears by cutting onions in front of an electric fan.

❀

Sprinkle dried onions on sandwiches prepared for lunch boxes. By lunchtime, they will have turned into crisp pieces of onion. This is especially helpful when some family members like onions, others do not.

❀

When large, sweet onions are about to go bad, make an onion cake: Shred 4 or 5 large onions; sauté slowly in butter until onions are transparent; drain on paper towels. Spread biscuit dough evenly over a medium-size cookie sheet. Sprinkle onions evenly over dough; salt and pepper to taste. Bake 15 to 20 minutes in a 400° F. oven.

❊

To speed the cooking of onions, broccoli stems, and Brussels sprouts, cut an X-like incision into the base.

❊

Add a lemon wedge to the pot when cooking cabbage or onions; this prevents the usual unpleasant odor.

❊

If only a small amount of pimiento is needed in preparing a dish, remove the centers from stuffed olives.

❊

As a stuffing for green peppers, mash meatloaf with grated American cheese; moisten with tomato juice.

❊

Perk up leftover squash by adding some maple syrup before reheating.

❊

When stewing tomatoes add some crumbled rye bread.

❊

Put the juice from canned, cooked tomatoes in ice cube trays. Once frozen, put the tomato juice cubes in plastic bags. Use cubes to ice tomato drinks and for cooking.

❀

Enhance the flavor of inexpensive tomato juice: Buy a 46-ounce can of it and transfer the juice to a refrigerator bottle. Add 1 green onion, chopped, and 1 stalk of celery, cut up. When the juice is poured, the spout holds the vegetables back but the drink that emerges is deliciously similar to the expensive one.

Salads

To keep lettuce and celery from turning brown in the refrigerator, wash, drain well and wrap in paper towels or newspaper before placing in the crisper. Also line the crisper with paper. The paper will absorb excess moisture and keep the vegetables fresh longer.

❀

Sweet-pickle juice is good in coleslaw, potato salad or fresh vegetable salad.

❀

Make a completely new salad by whirling any remaining gelatin salad in a blender with a little whipping cream or cream cheese. Refrigerate until set.

❀

Add vinegar or pickle juice to nearly empty mayonnaise jars; shake and use as a basis for sweet-sour cabbage or salad dressings.

❀

Save small bits of chicken, ham and roast beef to make a chef's salad. Add leftover cheese, hard-boiled eggs, tomatoes, lettuce and dressing.

❀

To garnish salads for company dinners, fill a pastry tube with mayonnaise and decorate as you would a cake.

Fruits

When apples become dry and tasteless, coax the flavor out by cutting them into pieces and sprinkling cider over them.

❀

Freeze apples especially for pies; line pie pans with plastic wrap, letting enough drape over the sides to completely wrap the apples. Cut apples into the lined pan and freeze. After the apples have frozen solid, lift them from the pans and stack them in the freezer; wash the pans and return them to the cupboard. When ready to bake, roll out fresh piecrust, unwrap the frozen apples and fit them right into the pan. Add sugar, spices and flour as usual and pop in the oven. Apples will not discolor in the freezer.

❀

Use maple syrup as a substitute for sugar when making applesauce or apple pie.

❀

For variety, add a little anise to sugar when baking apples.

❀

Put 1 teaspoonful of sweet-pickle juice in the center of apples before baking.

❀

After holidays, use up hard candies by adding to applesauce. Heat thoroughly. The candy gives the applesauce a spicy flavor.

❀

When bananas are on the verge of going bad, mash and freeze them for use later.

❀

When sorting huckleberries, put them on a table and sit before it with a wide pan on your lap. Carefully roll the berries toward the pan. The green berries, leaves and small twigs will stay on the table; the good berries will roll into the pan.

❀

When only a little lemon juice is needed, pierce the lemon with a skewer; the lemon will stay fresher than if cut.

❀

Orange juice left over from breakfast can be used as a flavoring for icings, gelatins, salad dressings and cakes.

❀

For year-round special seasoning, save lemon or orange peelings; dry them; pulverize in blender or

grate fresh and spread on a pie plate to dry 24 hours
on the back of the stove or on top of the radiator. Put
in a jar. The rinds will store indefinitely.

❀

When baking rhubarb, mix about a tablespoon of
flour or cornstarch in the sugar before sprinkling it
over the rhubarb.

❀

To save time when canning or freezing peaches, try
leaving the skins on—just wash and rub, the same
as with apricots. The peaches taste better and are
more nutritious.

❀

Bake fresh or canned peaches, or other fruits, in
sweet-pickle juice and use in compotes.

❀

Remove the core from pear halves with a melon
baller. The whole core comes out with one scoop.

❀

To make a flavorful, inexpensive substitute for
maple syrup, cover peach, pear or other fruit peelings
with water, then sweeten to taste and boil to the consistency of syrup. Use on pancakes or waffles.

❀

Save syrup from canned fruit to use when cooking
fresh fruits. The syrup adds flavor and saves on sugar.

❀

If interrupted when making jam, put the pitted
fruit into the freezer. Next morning, continue the

process, putting the berries through the food chopper while still frozen. The work will be cleaner—the berries will be easier to manage without losing one drop of juice.

Cakes, Cookies, Pies and Desserts

Cakes

For an upside-down cake, line the bottom and sides of the pan with foil. Put in melted butter, brown sugar and fruit and arrange in a pretty pattern. Pour in the cake batter and, when the cake is baked, turn it out onto a plate and peel off the foil. None of the topping will stick to the pan.

❀

Serve crumbly, messy cakes attractively—angel food cake with boiled frosting, for example—by slicing the entire cake before frosting and decorating. Use the decorations, such as rosettes, to hide slice marks.

❀

A quick and easy way to make a large birthday cake with only one cake mix: Use one nine-inch layer for a clown face and cut the other layer as illustrated. Use the edge of the baking pan to mark the bottom of the hat; it will be a perfect fit. Hold the pieces together with icing and decorate as desired.

❀

Cut stale angel food cake into ½″ slices; shape with cookie cutters; toast "cookies" for a few minutes; frost with confectioners'-sugar icing.

❀

Alternate slices of stale angel food cake with layers of strawberry and chocolate ice cream in a loaf pan; freeze.

❀

Cut stale angel food cake or sponge cake into cubes. Using a fork, dip into melted semi-sweet chocolate. Let extra chocolate drip into pan; roll cube in finely chopped nuts. Chill until firm. Serve with ice cream.

❀

Use an ice cream scoop to fill cupcake papers evenly, with no spilling around the edges.

❀

Slice leftover gingerbread into two layers; spread ginger conserve between the layers. Cut into squares, heat and top with whipped cream.

❀

When icing a many-layered cake, slide three sticks of dry spaghetti down through the layers. This will keep the layers from sliding before the icing sets.

❀

To split a layer of cake for torte or shortcake, simply pull a length of dental floss through it. Even a hot biscuit-type shortcake can be split this way without tearing.

❀

Use up leftover icing by spreading it between two plain biscuit cookies to make a cream sandwich.

❀

Save cake frosting in a cake decorator tube in the refrigerator. Use to decorate graham cracker cookies.

❀

To decorate cakes easily, follow this method: With a cookie cutter, make a light impression on a frosted cake; follow the lines of the impression with a pastry tube filled with frosting; fill in with colored sugar.

❀

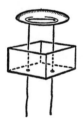

When transporting a cake, protect it from damage by using this method: Punch two holes in a paper plate and run a string through the holes; punch two corresponding holes in the bottom of a box. Put the cake on the paper plate and set it in the box. Pull string ends through the holes in the box and tie underneath.

❀

Make king-size cupcakes by using eight-ounce aluminum containers. Grease the cups; fill about a third full; bake on a cookie sheet. After frosting, snap on plastic lids and freeze for future use. Remove frozen cupcake and thaw. One cake mix makes about twelve king-size cupcakes.

❀

Make a nonreturnable cake dish by wrapping an old phonograph record in waxed paper.

❀

To keep waxed paper lining in place while pouring batter into cake pans, grease the sides of the baking dish lightly and press the paper against them.

Cookies

Keep cookies from burning on the bottom by cooling off the cookie sheet before baking each batch. Run cold water over the back of the sheet, so that the greased front will not be disturbed; dry the back; continue baking.

❀

Wash cookie sheets, cake tins, etc., while still warm; burned crumbs and sticky spots come off readily without any scouring.

❀

Slice ice-box-cookie dough with string held tautly in both hands.

❀

Delicate square cookies can be evenly cut by using a removable ice cube separator.

❀

To cut waxed paper for wrapping a large quantity of cookies individually: Take a knife and cut three sections around the roll without unwinding the paper; put the roll back in the box and use the cutter on the box to tear off three just-the-right-size pieces at a time.

❈

Use freezer paper when rolling out pie dough. It works much more effectively than waxed paper.

Pies

To prevent the bottom crust of fruit pies from becoming soggy, sprinkle dry bread crumbs on the crust before putting in the filling. For more flavor, use vanilla-wafer crumbs or finely ground nuts. The crumbs will take up much of the extra juice.

❈

When making coconut cream pies, put the coconut in the chilled baked crust instead of in the filling. The coconut absorbs moisture and keeps the piecrust crisper.

❈

To roll dough evenly: Break a yardstick in half; lay one half at each end of the pastry board or cloth so that the rolling pin rests on them.

❈

Sweet-pickle juice, used instead of water in piecrusts, is especially good for mincemeat and pumpkin pies. The crust will have added flavor and will turn a beautiful brown. As an alternative, add the juice to the mincemeat itself.

Desserts

When a scoop of ice cream is left, use it to make ice cream sandwiches. Soften the ice cream and spread it between two cookies; freeze.

❈

Put leftover servings of desserts—crumbled cookies, scoops of ice cream, a lone maraschino cherry—into parfait glasses kept in the freezer. When the glasses are full, serve as "surprise parfaits."

❈

Pack ice cream bought in bulk into small round plastic margarine dishes, then close with plastic covers and freeze. The containers stack well, provide individual servings and eliminate the messy job of dishing out ice cream.

❈

Use chocolate chips and a dash of mace in rice pudding, instead of cinnamon and raisins.

❈

Apple peelings simmered with two cloves and a stick of cinnamon and a tablespoon of honey make a good syrup for pancakes, or a sauce for puddings.

❈

Add a little unsweetened cocoa to flour before greasing and flouring baking tins so that cookies and cakes will not have a floury look.

❊

Use a baby-bottle warmer to melt shortening or chocolate quickly.

4.

Handyman's Hints
and Home Repairs

Painting and Plastering

When painting with a roller, line the tray with a plastic dry-cleaning bag before pouring in the paint. When the job is done, discard the liner; the tray will not have to be cleaned.

❀

To leave a paintbrush or roller for several days without it drying out, slip it into a plastic bag; twist the bag to remove air, and knot the bag.

❀

After painting, fill clean nail-polish or shoe-polish bottles with some of the leftover paint; label. Such containers—with brushes or daubers attached to the lids—are excellent for small touchups; they are also easier to store than large, almost-empty paint cans.

❀

Before storing paint, mark a line on the outside of the can to indicate its level: You can tell at a glance how much is left and what color is in the can.

❀

The lower half of a clean milk carton makes an excellent container for holding small amounts of paint or varnish. The straight side of the carton has a better wiping edge for the brush than the rim of a can.

❀

After painting a room, before replacing the light-switch plate, put a piece of masking tape on the inside of the plate; on the tape write the date the room was painted, the color of the paint, how many coats were used, and the quantity of paint used. When it is time to repaint, the information will be right at hand.

❀

When painting a woven wire fence, use a paint roller to save time and paint.

❀

Instead of puttying and then painting, do both jobs at once: Mix the putty with the paint.

❀

A quick way to repair holes in plaster and eliminate repainting the patch is to mix food coloring in the plaster to match the color of the walls.

❀

Use an empty window-cleaner spray bottle for damping the edges of plaster before patching: The spray will reach the deepest recesses of the broken plaster.

❀

For an even finish, apply stain to woodwork with cotton balls.

General Hints

When antique pine furniture is covered with old-fashioned red stain—a mixture of buttermilk and ink berries—it is impossible to remove with ordinary paint and varnish removers. To remove the stain, wet the entire piece with laundry bleach; wait at least fifteen minutes; then rub with steel wool. Repeat. Reapply bleach and let stand overnight; rinse with water the following day. The wood will be bleached without raising the grain.

❀

"Insulate" windows against cold or heat by hanging plastic linings behind draperies. The linings can be attached to the same hooks as the draperies.

❀

Smooth small nicks on drinking glasses by rubbing with #00 emery paper.

❀

Hide chips in a porcelain sink with contact paper, instead of liquid porcelain, which often yellows and peels off. Cut designs out of the contact paper and stick over chipped areas. The paper will stay firmly attached for months.

❀

Keep upholstered furniture away from walls by nailing a strip of wood to the floor about seven inches from the wall. The furniture stop will keep wallpaper and paint free of furniture marks.

❀

Replace the pulls on a child's dresser with building blocks.

❀

To limber up stubborn locks, dip key into graphite or machine oil; turn key in lock several times.

❀

If a key keeps getting stuck in the lock and you have no graphite at hand, pour the contents of your pencil sharpener over the key or rub it with the lead from a pencil.

❀

For easy identification of keys, paint the top of each one to match the car, the front door, etc.

❀

Remove the bottom screws of towel-rack brackets and replace them with cup hooks. Sew loops on small towels and washcloths; hang them from the hooks.

❀

Make a gadget for retrieving things from hard-to-reach places: Attach a cup hook to the end of a three- or four-foot dowel (or use the handle of a worn-out mop or broom).

❀

To seal a small hole in a window screen, dot the hole with clear cement glue. The repair will be unnoticeable.

❀

Fill in holes or gashes in linoleum with a thick paste made by mixing shellac with small particles of linoleum that have been scraped off a matching piece.

After applying, allow paste to harden; sandpaper smooth, and then wax entire surface.

❊

A hairdryer makes an excellent fireplace bellows.

❊

Use a hairdryer to thaw a frozen water pipe.

❊

Shut-off valves on water pipes, such as those leading from the hot-water heater, should be turned every six months to keep them from sticking so that, in case of an emergency, they will always be in working order.

❊

To cut down noise in the home, apply self-sticking protective pads to side edges and corners of cabinet doors. The hardest slam will be reduced to a dull thud.

❊

Apartment dwellers who like their music full volume or those who have hearing defects can avoid disturbing other tenants or members of the family by using earphones. Electricians will install jacks quickly and inexpensively in anything from a television set to an electric organ.

❊

To prevent container openings from sticking, particularly on nail-polish bottles, tubes of glue, cans of varnish, nonaerosol hair spray, etc., rub petroleum jelly inside the cover and on the grooves before using for the first time.

❊

Snow will easily slide off a shovel coated with floor wax.

❀

Use a large, old strainer for sprinkling sand on an icy, slippery sidewalk; the job will go quicker, and the sand will be more evenly distributed than if thrown by hand.

❀

A garbage can will stay firmly anchored if it is placed inside an old car tire.

❀

Coat a new garbage can with a primer for galvanized ware, then enamel it to match the trim on the house. The can will last longer and the visual results will enhance the yard.

❀

Make an attractive, inexpensive desk: Nail four wooden fruit boxes together in pairs to make two sections. Nail a plywood sheet, or boards, across the two sections; paint the desk to match room decor. Glue linoleum across the plywood top for a smooth desk top.

5.

Gardening

Indoor Plants and Flowers

Make an attractive rod for hanging plants in a window. Buy drapery brackets that extend several inches from the wall, a sturdy dowel, and two decorative finials. Paint the dowel and attach it, with the hardware, to the wall above the drapes. The plants will not interfere with opening and closing the curtains.

❀

Keep the base of a broken canister vacuum cleaner: It makes an excellent, movable stand for a heavy plant.

❀

A rusty, discarded barbecue can be spray painted and used as an indoor or outdoor stand for plants.

❀

Fill a cracked birdbath with soil and plant low-growing flowers and trailing ivy in it. Use indoors or outside.

❀

A discarded television stand makes a decorative and practical holder for houseplants and can be moved easily to catch the sun.

❀

For kitchen greenery, cut half an inch off carrot, beet or turnip tops, and place in a dish with pebbles and a little water. Onions and hearts of celery will sprout in jars with water at the bottom. In addition to their decorative effect, the tops of the plants can be cut off for use in salads and soups.

❀

Plant a few unpeeled garlic cloves in a flowerpot, blunt end down, and just barely cover the cloves with good potting soil. In a few weeks' time, fresh, tasty green shoots will appear—grown on the kitchen windowsill. Snip and use in stews, soups or tossed salads. The plants will last for months.

❀

Give young children coriander seeds to plant in a flowerpot: They sprout quickly and in no time the germinating leaves give way to the curly leaves in the center of the plant. Planting herbs from seed is both a delightful way for children to participate in kitchen activities and also a great source for gift-giving.

❀

Houseplant trellises can be made from plastic tomato containers. Cut off one side of the container and stick it into the soil. For a larger trellis, cut off more than one side and weave the pieces together.

❀

Clip spring clothespins on a flat stick to make an instant, miniature flowerpot trellis.

❀

Make a natural insecticide: Fill a jar with water,

add onions and garlic and let it sit several days to a week. Then spray plants with the water.

Do not throw eggshells away: Put them in a large jar and fill with water. Use to water houseplants.

Make "frogs" for floral arrangements from plastic pint vegetable baskets, the kind that hold cherry tomatoes and fruit: Cut baskets down to fit containers; turn them upside down and insert flower stems in the mesh slots.

A clay drain tile makes a rustic vase for displaying dried leaves, grass and flowers; it can be purchased for pennies at a lumberyard.

To arrange flowers whose stems are too short, stick stems in plastic straws, then cut straws to desired length.

To hold up short-stemmed flowers, pour several inches of bird gravel into a glass vase. Add water as usual and arrange flowers in the vase.

For a perfect flower arrangement when the mouth of a vase is too wide, place narrow strips of transparent gummed tape across the mouth to make a small opening in the center for a few flowers, or make several openings by crisscrossing tape to hold in position a dozen or more long stems. The tape is practically invisible and can be soaked off the vase when desired.

❀

To keep a corsage fresh and perky for several hours, wrap the flower stems with a piece of wet cotton, then cover the cotton with transparent gummed tape.

❀

On bright, sunny days, place sheets of tissue over African violets while the sun is brightest. This protects the foliage from burning and spotting.

❀

A bunch of decorative rhododendron leaves, purchased at the florist shop, can be kept fresh for five to six months instead of the usual six weeks. Change the water every two weeks, clean the vase thoroughly and break an inch off the bottom of each branch before replacing it into the fresh water. This not only revives the leaves that have drooped, but often results in the growth of new ones. As the bunch grows shorter, use lower bowls and vases to suit.

Outdoor Gardening

To achieve a more even distribution when sowing small seeds, use a salt shaker. Sprinkling the seeds from the shaker prevents bunching; more plants will reach maturity.

❀

To avoid disturbing seedlings, use a funnel to pour water through a drinking straw stuck into the soil at the base of the plants.

❀

Use an old whisk broom to water delicate seedlings: Dip the broom in water and sprinkle the plants lightly.

❀

To sprout seeds in winter turn your car into a mini greenhouse. Put a small seedbed in the sunlight on the dashboard—a good alternative for those without sunny windows.

❀

To start outdoor plants from seed, an inexpensive seed nursery, small enough for a windowsill, can be made from a cardboard box. Using a sharp knife, cut the top off; then cut the four sides and bottom one inch from the edges, creating a framework with four legs. Turn upside down; cover with plastic wrap, taped or stapled at the corners. Place seedling containers on a tray; cover with the "greenhouse."

❀

When cutting roses with thorny stems, hold the stem with a spring clothespin.

❀

To protect newly planted saplings from small children, get them involved: Plan a tree-planting ceremony and invite all of the children who play in your yard. Name each sapling after a child. Thereafter, each will protect his own tree from the others.

❀

Small bushes can be protected during cold spells by covering with overturned bushel baskets. To anchor the baskets, put an old-fashioned clothespin over each wire handle and push them into the ground.

❀

After weeding a lawn with a digger, fill holes with a mixture of grass seed, fine topsoil and peat moss.

❀

To rid the lawn of tenacious weeds without leaving holes in the lawn, use an apple corer. Insert the serrated edge of the corer at the base of each weed and lift it out.

❀

To eliminate bare spots under shade trees, try planting moss gathered in clumps from the woods. Loosen the soil, lay the clumps on top, water well and wait for the moss to spread into a velvety green carpet.

❀

Make a garden of night-blooming white flowers—well known for their fragrance and beauty—under bedroom windows or near a much-used summer porch or patio. Include such dependable, old-fashioned plants as nicotianas, annual babies'-breath, geraniums, petunias, moonflowers and alyssum.

❀

If the ends of a bamboo rake are worn, soak rake in very hot water for five minutes; then bend the ends under with pliers.

❀

For leveling spaded dirt into even rows, push an empty thread spool onto each of the two end teeth of the garden rake before raking.

❀

Make ties for tomato and other plants from old pantyhose or stockings cut lengthwise. The ties are sturdy, and will not cut into tender stalks.

❀

Mark the location of bulbs with colored plastic toothpicks, color-coded to the blossoms. This makes easier the rearrangement of flowerbeds after spring foliage has died back.

❀

For easy location and identification of bulbs and seeds, make garden markers from plastic gallon bleach containers. Cut container with sharp tin shears; label markers with a marking pen. The markers will not rust and the inscriptions will stay for months.

❀

Take the guesswork out of measuring insecticides, weed killers, or other chemicals—which can be harmful as well as wasteful—by keeping a set of measuring cups and spoons wherever garden supplies are stored.

❀

Make a handy depth gauge for planting by painting rings one inch apart on the handle of the garden trowel in contrasting colors.

❈

After gardening, tie trash such as large bundles of branches with old pantyhose; they make strong elastic ropes.

❈

For many gardening purposes, save cylindrical ice cream containers, milk cartons and large fruit-juice cans. Use cartons as starter-pots for rooting plants or for starting seeds; cut them away without disturbing roots when plants are ready for transplanting. Use cans for flowerpots; simply punch holes in the bottoms. When painted and decorated, cans also make good, disposable containers for taking flowers to the hospital.

❈

When painting flowerpots, just turn them upside down over a tin can, which acts as a stand and may be turned as the pot is painted. Leave pots on cans until dry.

❈

Wear garden gloves turned inside out—with seams on the outside, dirt will not stick so easily to the inside, and having the smoother surface next to the hands helps prevent work blisters.

❈

To avoid bringing garden dirt and bugs into your kitchen, make a sieve-like container for gathering garden vegetables: Replace the bottom of a wooden box with screening and attach a rope handle to the wooden sides. Spray the freshly gathered vegetables with a hose and the dirt will run out the bottom.

❁

Make a garden file. Write the common name for each plant in your garden on the outside of an envelope. Enclose a file card with pertinent information—type of soil plant prefers; best location; type of fertilizer and when applied; diseases common to the plant. When the plants go to seed, empty pods into the envelopes, for planting the following year.

❁

In new neighborhoods where many residents are starting gardens from scratch, pool orders for plants and shrubs—nurseries offer better prices when plants are ordered in quantity.

❁

Make an all-weather cover for a garden umbrella by cutting and stitching oilcloth into a cone. At night or during bad weather, simply close the umbrella and slip the cover on.

❁

Make a lovely garden house for summer evening entertaining or for a child's playhouse: Set five posts in the ground—one at each corner and one to allow for a door. Cover the top and sides with chicken wire; plant morning glories, silver lace, or other fast-growing vines around the base.

❁

Turn the eyesore of an unused swing set into a lovely addition to the backyard. Hang flower baskets from the frame; attach a bird feeder to the overhead bar; plant flowering vines to trail up the legs.

Backyard Bird Watching

Prepare cantaloupe seeds for bird feeding stations as follows: Let the seeds stand in a bowl of water overnight; in the morning put them in a colander under a stream of running water; then spread seeds on a cloth to dry. Store seeds in jars for year-round use.

❀

For feeding birds in cold climates, make winterized seed cakes: During the summer, freeze melon seeds in empty egg cartons. When the thermometer drops, take cakes out of the freezer and use when needed.

❀

Instead of discarding a cotton string mop, leave it outside for the birds during early spring. They will pick out the strands for nest-building.

❀

To attract birds to your garden, provide nest-building materials: When cleaning out your sewing basket or the lint trap of the dryer, collect bits of string, yarn and lint, and fasten to a tree or fence.

❀

Coax birds out of hiding during scorching summer months by turning on a fine-spray hose for several hours in one place on the lawn. In no time, the birds will return for a cooling bath.

✿

When making bread, also make a treat for the birds: Using any yeast recipe that forms a crust, roll dough into two logs, twist together, and shape into a circle. Press any type of seeds—sunflower, honey-dew, sesame, etc.—into the dough before baking. When the wreath is cool, hang it from a ribbon on a tree.

✿

In cold climates, press wild-bird seed and bread crumbs into a snowman; replenish him every few days.

✿

A seldomly used umbrella table can easily be turned into a bird feeding station. Simply stick a tree limb into the center hole of the table; from the branches, suspend grapefruit-rind halves that have been filled with bird feed.

✿

Make bird feeders or birdbaths out of large plastic bottles. Cut round holes in the side of each bottle; wash thoroughly; fill with water or bird feed; hang the containers from trees. The bottles can also be decorated with decals.

✿

Make tiny bird feeders out of individual cups cut from egg cartons. Fill the cups with suet, seeds or a mixture of peanut butter and graham cracker crumbs, and tack them (using only thumbtacks with painted tops) to porch posts or on window frames.

❀

A bird feeder made from natural materials—pine cones, evergreen boughs, etc.—will often attract birds when store-bought containers fail.

❀

Teach children that birds are their friends by keeping a "scrap sack": After meals, let the children put crumbs, apple cores and scraps into a paper sack to take outside and feed to the birds.

❀

Make a stable outdoor drinking dish. Use an angel-food-cake pan and drive a stick through the center hole.

6.

Home Sewing

General Sewing Hints

Make a sewing scrapbook: On the pages of a note-book, tape a piece of material and an extra button or two for every garment you make. If a button is lost, or a garment needs patching, the necessary materials will be at hand.

❀

Store used patterns in plastic bags instead of trying to fit them back into the envelopes.

❀

A shoe box is the perfect size for keeping patterns organized and "filed" upright.

❀

To prevent favorite patterns from ripping and to keep them wrinkle-free, spray with fabric spray.

❀

Repair torn patterns with plastic-coated freezer paper. Place paper under the torn area of pattern and press with a warm iron.

❀

Save the backing from self-adhesive coverings. The backings are usually ruled in one-inch squares and can be used to enlarge patterns.

❀

To enlarge patterns, draw a one-inch grid with a felt-tip pen on a large piece of cardboard. Place tissue paper over the cardboard; the lines show through clearly, making the enlargement easy.

❀

Cover old hemline marks with rows of zigzag stitching.

❀

When hemming café curtains, use floral cotton strips as edging, rather than expensive braided trim.

❀

Save on sewing accessories: Scan thrift shops and rummage sales for articles with unusual buttons and trimmings.

❀

Save scraps with selvage edges. Use in place of seam binding.

❀

Suspend pieces of a garment from a grip-type skirt hanger when you must stop in the middle of sewing. The fabric will stay clean and wrinkle-free.

❀

When hand-sewing and unable to find a thimble, wrap the end of your index finger with two Band-Aids —one across the top of the finger, one around the finger. This emergency thimble can be reused.

❀

Keep a dozen needles, threaded with often-used colors for last-minute repairs, in the sewing basket.

❀

If your sewing box is a mess from loose spools and tangled thread, color the ends of the spools with a pen or crayon which corresponds to the color of the thread. Stand the spools on end in orderly rows and you can choose at a glance the color of thread you need.

❀

An egg carton makes a useful storage space for spools of thread.

❀

Keep a small magnet in your sewing box and use it to pick up pins that fall to the floor during sewing sessions and to pick up the strays in the bottom of the box.

❀

When lengthening a soft wool garment, remove the old crease in this fashion: Place the garment right side up on the ironing board; put a piece of heavy twine on the crease; press over the twine with a steam iron.

❀

When making infant clothes that are buttoned down to the hemline, sew an extra button under the hem for use when the garment must be lengthened.

❀

When unable to match thread with an odd-colored fabric, look in the embroidery floss section of notions departments, where there is often a greater variety of shades and tints.

❀

Make bias strips to cover slipcover cording: For 18 yards of 1½" bias, use a 30" square of fabric. Fold fabric diagonally and cut on the fold. Place selvages together; stitch; press seam open. The material will then be an enormous bias strip. Lay this on the wrong side; fold into a square by bringing together the two original straight sides, mismatching the pieces so that 1½" extend on each end of the seam. Stitch and press seam open. Slip this cylinder of material over the end of the ironing board and, using a sewing gauge, begin cutting where the 1½" of material extend at one end of the seam.

❀

Keep a paper bag by the sewing machine for collecting small scraps. Use scraps for stuffed toys and throw pillows.

❀

Put a portable sewing machine on a piece of foam rubber, about an inch and a half thick and two inches wider than the machine base. The pad keeps the machine from "walking," absorbs vibration and makes a good pincushion.

❀

When synthetic fiber threads unwind too quickly and wrap around the sewing machine spindle, control the flow of the thread by encasing the spool in a one-inch-wide ring cut from a toilet paper roll. Slip the ring over the spool; then thread the machine, with the thread coming over the top rim of the cardboard ring. The flow of the thread will be slowed.

❀

A sponge, glued to the sewing machine base, makes a handy pincushion.

❀

Keep bias seams from stretching or sagging by stitching two rows ¼″ apart; do not open seam, but press to one side. The skirt will stay even at the hemline.

❀

Make a professional-looking collar with this tip: Staystitch ⅝″ from the edge of the under collar; make a ½″ allowance on the upper collar. When joining the pieces, ease the two rows of stitching together and make the seam exactly on them. Because of the extra ⅛″ on the upper part, the collar will roll under smoothly when turned.

❀

A toy ironing board set up next to the sewing machine is less cumbersome than a regular-size board. As you work, you can reach over and press out seams, darts, etc., without leaving your chair. Its small size is also handy for ironing such things as sleeves on children's clothes.

❀

To help thread a sewing machine, keep a piece of cardbard—black on one side, white on the other—in your sewing basket. Put the cardboard under the needle when threading. Use the dark side for light thread, the light side for dark thread. The contrast will make it easier to see the thread.

❀

When the bottoms have stretched on nylon or acrylic sweaters, put elastic thread on the sewing machine bobbin. Sew along the bottom edge of the sweater, right side up, so that the elastic thread will be on the underside. Make as many rows as needed.

❀

To eliminate tangling and knotting, apply wax to cotton thread when sewing by hand or machine. To wax thread: String several spools of thread together through center holes; soak in melted wax for five minutes. Remove spools from wax and wipe them with paper towels.

❀

If you use the sewing machine often for hemming or putting in a seam, keep handy a box of cut strips for rag rugs or patches for a quilt; as you finish a project, sew a few patches or strips together before putting the machine away.

❀

When covering a button with silk or a sheer fabric, make a neater job by first covering the button with wool or flannel.

❀

Buttons stay on longer if the thread is coated with clear nail polish. Do not use on rayon-acetate fabrics.

❀

Prevent coat buttons from falling off by fastening them on with round millinery elastic, found in notions departments. Draw one of the metal ends through the material from the wrong side; leave 1″ extending on the underside. Thread once through two holes of a four-buttonhole button; leave a ½″ shank when drawing the thread back to the underside; leave 1″ extending and tie the two ends into a knot. Repeat the process for the other two holes of the button. After knotting the ends, double knot both pieces of elastic together. The button will have "give" and will not rip off.

❀

Small waxed shoelaces make professional-looking button loops. They come in white, black and brown. Following the pattern procedure, attach the laces to the material. Even those who have no difficulty making loops will find this method a time-saver.

❀

Before using an old zipper, spray with starch and press; it will go in like new.

❀

Keep the rough underside of a buttonhole attachment from snagging fabric. Put plastic wrap over the fabric; sew the buttonhole through the plastic; rip the plastic off when done.

Mending Techniques

Mend torn corners of fitted sheets by cutting pieces of old white socks and placing them over the holes, then stitching them flat. The knitted fabric has enough give to stretch over the mattress without further tearing.

❀

When hem-stitched sheets and pillowcases are worn at the hem joinings, cut the hems off, rip them open, dye (for a border effect) and sew back on as blind hems.

❀

When a fitted sheet wears thin in the middle, leaving the sides and ends in good condition, stitch a mattress pad to the sheet, thus making the pad a fitted one while keeping it smooth and in place.

❀

Sew a wide strip of unbleached muslin along the edge of a blanket too short for a bed; the muslin tucks in out of sight and holds the blanket firmly in place.

❀

Use transparent tape, instead of pins, when appliquéing or mending garments and linens with patches.

❀

Keep a "repairs basket" next to the sewing machine. Never start a new project without first mending at least two articles from the basket.

❀

Keep a straight wooden clothespin in the sewing basket to stick inside the fingers of gloves that need mending.

❀

Pull snags in polyester doubleknit through to the underside with a wire needle threader. Push the threader through the fabric from the underside. The threader will not split the thread, as would a crochet hook.

❀

Keep children's pants from bagging and wearing at the knees by applying an iron-on patch to the inside of the pants leg at the knee.

❀

Use iron-on corduroy patches to reinforce the feet of children's pajamas.

❀

Bind worn coat edges and pockets with grosgrain ribbon.

❀

When a new suit is being tailored, ask for the scraps: They will come in handy later for mending, or for taking along on shopping expeditions for matching shirts, ties or other accessories.

❀

Use cotton swabs as shirt-collar stays. They are the perfect length, they keep collars firm and the padded tips will not wear out collar material.

❀

Use iron-on tape to mend buttonholes when corners have been slashed too far. Press tape over the mistake and recut the buttonhole.

❀

To replace the hobs on a hobnail bedspread, wrap lightweight cotton thread about a dozen times around fork tines; then sew to the spread through the center tines. Clip to desired shape and length.

✸

After slipcover material is pinned on the chair, remove it and fold over on the lines of the pins. Steam iron. This gives a distinct line where the stitching will be, even if pins drop out while stitching. When you are ready to add the ruffle, put the slipcover back on the chair and use a skirt straightener set to the correct number of inches.

Recycling Clothes

Cut the elastic waistbands off worn pantyhose for reuse in slacks, shorts, etc.

✸

When children's pajama feet wear out, replace them with potholders, using the type with asbestos on one side—the asbestos makes a durable sole. Simply trace the child's feet on the potholders, cut them out and sew the potholder-feet to the pajamas with the cloth side next to the foot.

✸

To extend use, add ruffles or colorful trim to the legs of outgrown pajamas.

✸

Save old leather gloves for reinforcing elbows and edges of sleeves and pockets of children's clothes.

❀

When the cuffs on a child's jacket give out, make new ones from pieces cut from old knee socks; fold the sock material in half and stitch it onto the jacket.

❀

Lengthen the outgrown arms of a snowsuit by sewing on a pair of woolen wristlets.

❀

Make bodyshirts for children: Cut elastic off outgrown underpants and sew underpants to the shirttail. Slit the crotch; reinforce with seam binding; attach two snaps.

❀

Make small, soft washcloths for babies from old T-shirts: cut 3″ x 5″ pieces of the material; use double thicknesses; zigzag stitch around the edges.

❀

Work a row of loose single crochet around each washcloth (bedspread cotton is a good weight) and at each corner crochet a hanging loop. The edging adds body and wear to the cloth and the loops make it easy to hang up the washcloth.

❀

When a baby outgrows his blanket sleepers, open the bottom seam and use for beach cover-ups: The thick material will dry and warm the child quickly.

❀

If a toddler's one-piece snowsuit is outgrown, but the shoulders still fit, cut it off at the crotch and hem it to make a good play jacket.

❀

Make pants for chores that require working on your knees by sewing small pockets on the knees of pants and cutting foam sponges to fit inside.

❀

Convert an outgrown pullover sweater into a cardigan. Cut the pullover down the center front, and overcast the edges with needle and thread. Then crochet an edge down both sides of the front and around the neck.

❀

Make a fringed poncho from a wool carriage blanket no longer in use. Fold blanket in half, right sides together. Mark the center of the folded edge. Starting there, cut a 3″ slit in both directions, making a 6″ opening. At each end of the opening, cut a 2″ slit so that you can turn the fabric back. Turn fabric back; pin; and stitch around opening.

❀

Hunt for pleated wool skirts in thrift shops—one skirt will make a warm and colorful shirt. Take out all seams and press the material flat. Use the waistband for cuffs; arrange the shirt pattern on the material so that the skirt hemline becomes the shirt's hem.

❀

Make a sleeveless maternity smock. Cut the sleeves off long-sleeved shirts and slit the sleeves open. Gather, or box pleat, one end of the material. Then slit open the shirt at side seams and insert the pleated or gathered material.

❀

Make inexpensive maternity pants by cutting the fronts out of your pants from seam to seam and replacing them with the stretchy tops of old pantyhose. This works well with blue jeans, as well as other types of pants.

❀

Make heavy-duty potholders from worn blue jeans. Cut jeans below the knee; tuck top half of piece into the lower half. Stitch around the sides.

❀

Make a washable and attractive case for sunglasses from a pretty potholder: Fold it in half and stitch across the bottom and up one side.

❀

Turn worn washrags into potholders. Fold washrags in half; lay them on a piece of fabric 1″ wider all around. Fold the fabric edges in, making a finished edge; then fold the whole thing in half and stitch around the edges. (Optional: Stitch rickrack around the edges, making a loop at one corner for hanging the potholder.)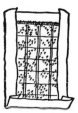

❀

When towels are worn, cut them into squares, fold over, and stitch on three sides to make mitten washrags.

❀

Before throwing away blue jeans, cut out the good portions. When enough denim has been collected, machine stitch the irregular patches together to make a sturdy beach blanket.

❀

Use leftover material scraps to make an infant's bib. Cut the bib to shape and line it with an old terrycloth towel or plastic tablecloth cut to size, then stitch up the edges with seam binding, by hand or by machine. Attach snaps or excess seam binding ties as fasteners.

❀

Make two canvas bags from an old army duffel bag by following the pattern of a regular paper shopping bag. Outside pockets and handles of several thicknesses can be made from leftover material. Insert a heavy piece of cardboard, cut to fit, inside the bottom of each bag for reinforcement.

❀

Sew a pillowcase from a man's worn cotton shirt: Cut off tails and top section at the underarms; remove buttons and save for other sewing ventures. Sew closed *one* of the open ends of the shirt as well as the button panel. Leave pocket on for storage of little items such as tissues.

❀

Before discarding old handbags with zipper compartments, cut out the lining very carefully, rip out the zippers and use them in dressmaking.

7.

Needlework, Crafts and Decorating Ideas

Yarn, Thread and Embroidery

When working with two or more balls of yarn or thread, put the balls in a plastic bag with small holes, such as potatoes come in. Thread yarn through the holes. The yarn will stay clean and untangled throughout the project.

❀

Wear a cobbler's apron to prevent tangling when you are working with two balls of yarn: Use an end pocket for each ball. Put work in the center pocket when interrupted.

❀

To smooth yarn for reuse: Pull a coat hanger into a square; wind yarn around it; suspend over a pot of steaming water for two minutes.

❀

When storing balls of wool, pull a strand of yarn out of each, and tape the end to the side of the box—at a glance you will know what colors you have on hand.

❀

Fasten spare strands of wool onto the back of a finished needlepoint project; the additional yarn may come in handy for future repairs.

❀

Use the plastic holders from soft-drink six-packs to sort yarns when working on a crewel project. Knot yarn over the plastic, as if you were adding fringe.

❧

To ease threading a tapestry or rug needle with yarn, cut a strip of paper two inches long and slightly narrower than the needle eye. Fold paper in half, around a strand of yarn; pass the short ends of the paper through the eye, drawing the yarn through.

❧

Prevent fabric from stretching when you are embroidering by ironing lightweight iron-on facing to the back.

❧

Make embroidery hoops from plastic containers for margarine. Cut out the center of the lid, leaving the rim; then cut the center of the container bottom away from its rim. The two rims snapped together form the hoop.

❧

Keep embroidery floss from tangling as you work by winding it around a sponge hair curler; the plastic clip will keep it from unwinding. One large curler can hold several different colors of thread.

❧

Your favorite embroidery transfers can produce good clear prints again and again if you renew the lines with a good (not too waxy) crayon before pressing the other side with a hot iron.

❧

Have your child draw pictures on pillow-size pieces of needlepoint tapestry. The finished "picture pillow" makes a lovely gift for grandparents and may be personalized with the child's initials and the date.

❀

To keep needlepoint yarns organized and untangled, attach small screw eyes into the lower edge of a light wood coat hanger and draw strands of wool, cut to 18″ lengths, through the eyes.

Knitting and Crochet

When casting on knitting stitches, cast over two needles. The first row will be looser and easier to work with.

❀

An ideal storage place for knitting needles is an empty aluminum-foil box.

❀

After knitting a garment for a growing child, wind the leftover yarn in a hank, tie loosely and launder each time the garment is washed. The yarn will stay the same color as the garment and can be used for lengthening sleeves or mending.

❀

Sew seams of children's knitted sweaters with a shade of wool slightly darker than the garment. When the child outgrows the sweater and you want to reuse the yarn, you will be able to find the strand of wool joining the seams and avoid cutting into the garment by mistake.

❀

When binding off a series of stitches on a sweater shoulder, knit or purl up to the bound-off stitches, slipping the last one. When binding off the next series you will find that the line will be smoother and will not have the usual "stair step" appearance.

❀

Transfer long columns of printed crochet and knitting instructions onto 3″ x 5″ cards, three or four numbered rows to each card. Hold the stack together with a rubber band. When the directions on the top card are completed, move the card to the bottom of the deck. Leave off work after each top card is completed; no more risk of losing your place in directions when you work on complicated patterns in spare moments.

❀

Knit while listening to music: You will unconsciously knit to the rhythm and the finished piece will be very even.

❀

As sizes are not indicated on circular knitting needles, mark them with nail polish: Apply four stripes of polish on a size 4 needle; five on a size 5 needle, etc.

❀

When teaching a left-handed individual to knit, let the person follow your movements in a mirror.

❀

When interrupted while knitting or crocheting, prevent slipped stitches by clipping a clothespin over work and needles.

❈

When knitting a cardigan, achieve a firmer front edge, on which it is possible to use a heavier button without misshaping the sweater, by following this method: Carry an attached ball of yarn and use two threads for the edge stitch; drop one thread and continue across pattern.

❈

To achieve a cleaner, firmer edge when knitting with fine yarn, knit in the back, rather than the front, of the first row (cast-on stitches).

❈

When knitting, put the skein of yarn in an old stocking. This provides just the right tension to keep the yarn flowing smoothly while preventing tangles.

❈

Knit scrap-yarn mittens that small children will love to wear: Cut strands of leftover yarn in half, tie scraps together, wind into two balls (one for each mitten) and watch the "mystery" color scheme unfold as you knit.

❈

Make a neat binding for knitted buttonholes by making a small, inverted box pleat in the grosgrain ribbon behind each buttonhole. Buttonhole-stitch the folded ribbon edges.

❈

Leave starting threads long when knitting Argyle socks; later you can sew up the back seam with them, matching the colors as you work.

❃

Place a safety pin after each 10 or 20 stitches when a knitting pattern calls for working with a large number of stitches—the pins will help in counting.

❃

Knit with two different-colored needles—one color representing the odd numbers in the pattern, the other for the even numbers.

❃

Make tiny knitting needles to ease the task of working with several needles on small areas, such as cables or the thumbs of children's mittens. Break two plastic needles in half, so that each piece is about 2½″ long; sandpaper ends to smooth points or run through a pencil sharpener. The small needles are less clumsy than regular-size needles.

❃

When giving hand-knitted gifts, enclose a label from the yarn used; this provides useful information such as washing instructions.

❃

Place a plastic toothbrush holder in your sewing cabinet for crochet hooks of various sizes.

❃

Instead of making a long chain when starting filet crochet, try this method: Chain 5, turn; double in first stitch of chain. You now have your first space made; chain 5, turn, double in third stitch of first chain (second space made). Make required number of spaces for the first row and go on from there with the second row of the design.

❀

When crocheting a base chain, use a hook two sizes larger than necessary: This keeps the edge from being too tight.

❀

Crochet shoelaces to match handmade knitted sweaters and socks. Make a chain measuring 24″–26″ in length, when stretched. Wrap each end tightly with an inch of transparent tape, for easy threading through the eyes of the shoe.

Quilting and Patchwork

Cut quilting patterns from sandpaper: The sandpaper holds material securely as you cut from the pattern. Cutting through the sandpaper also sharpens scissors.

❀

Drive a headless nail into the edge of a quilting frame to hold a spool of thread: It will always be within reach.

❀

Quilt with hoops so that you can quilt anywhere, even while relaxing in bed. Prepare the quilt for this method as follows: Stretch the lining, seams up, on the floor, and lightly tack the edges to the floor at 12″ intervals. Spread cotton batting evenly on the lining. Place the top over this, stretching wrinkles out, using safety pins to pin the top to the lining just inside each tack. Then pin top, cotton batting and lining together all over the quilt. Space safety pins 12″ apart. Remove tacks. As in regular quilting, start working in the center. As hoops are placed for working, remove pins and ease wrinkles out.

❀

Instead of repeatedly tracing the same pattern for appliquéd quilts, try this method: Draw or trace the pattern onto a swatch once; place this swatch on top of a small stack of pieces to be traced; then stitch on the sewing machine, with no thread in the needle, along the pencil line. This gives a perforated, easy-to-follow cutting line on all pieces and saves much time.

❀

After sewing a garment for a child, gather scraps and cut into squares. Save the blocks and make into a "memory quilt" when the child is grown.

❀

Cut out the best part of an old, faded quilt and use as a child's crib cover. On the backing of the quilt, embroider the names of the child's friends, using various colors of leftover embroidery floss.

❀

Make beautiful, patchwork draperies for pennies: Cut sewing scraps into squares, join them together on the sewing machine and line them with white sheets.

❀

Make colorful wall panels with pieces of inherited patchwork. Mount the patchwork on a solid, neutral background—such as gunmetal taffeta—and frame.

❀

Make appliqué patterns from children's picture books or coloring books: The designs are large, simple and easy to trace.

Rugmaking

Wet wool material or other loosely woven fabrics before tearing them into strips for hooked or braided rugs. Wetting the fabric eliminates lint. Dry the strips before using them.

❀

Small, woven rugs will last longer if you sew each end on the machine with a row of V-shaped stitching about four inches deep; this will prevent fraying and will make the rug stronger.

❀

Save time when joining strips for a rag rug: Sew ends of two strips together; fasten thread firmly, but do not clip. Sew on the next strip and draw it close to the first ones. Continue in this manner until enough have been joined, then clip the unnecessary connecting threads so that the whole strip lies flat. This eliminates stopping to clip and knot threads each time strips are joined.

❀

Keep scissors firmly in place when hooking a rug on a frame by hanging them on a drapery hook pinned to the rug canvas.

❀

To achieve a tighter surface when hooking rugs, use screw eyes, instead of thumbtacks, to attach rug to the frame.

❀

When cutting strips of material for hooked rugs, stop cutting about ¼″ from the edge; this keeps the strips together and makes it easy to snip the strips off one at a time when ready to use.

❀

When making a hooked rug, instead of transferring patterns to the burlap, iron the design onto a thin, transparent material, such as organdy; baste the material to the burlap; hook through both. The design will be clearer, less blurred.

❀

While hooking a rug, keep the various strips of colored material in separate paper bags. Roll the bags down at the top, forming little box-like sacks, and pack them into an open carton. When the rug is finished, unroll the sack tops and tie them with a strip of the material inside, so that when needed again, you will know how much material and variety of color you have for your next rug.

❀

Make braided rugs or bathmats from old pantyhose and stockings. Bleach them before using: This softens the various colors so that they will blend nicely.

❀

Make braided rugs that do not require sewing together. Fasten a safety pin to the end of one strip of material; begin braiding. When the braid is a few inches long, take the strip with the safety pin and bend it around clockwise, as you would to start sewing. Loop it through one strip of finished braid. Continue braiding, stopping every few inches to "sew" the just-finished braid onto the growing main part of the rug.

Crafts and Decorating Ideas

Make stringing beads easier by dipping the ends of the thread into clear nail polish—the beads will slip easily over the stiffened ends.

❀

Make "needles" for stringing beads by rolling the ends of string in transparent tape.

❀

Use frogs as fasteners on macramé necklaces.

❀

Prevent macramé cords from tangling as you work by wrapping the individual cords around your hand

and binding with a wire twist. The twist makes it easy to lengthen the cords as needed.

❀

Put colorful autumn leaves between waxed paper and press with a warm iron. The leaves will last longer.

❀

Make cards, bookmarks or pictures with pressed flowers. Mount blossoms on paper and cover with self-adhesive clear vinyl.

❀

Using clear plastic fishing line, hang prisms at varying heights for an unusual window treatment. Buy inexpensive triangular prisms from scientific supply houses; use old decanter tops or prisms from chandeliers. When the sun strikes the glass, the room will become alive wtih color.

❀

Save cards received upon the birth of your baby to decorate items in the nursery. Cut the designs out; pink the edges; and paste onto lampshades, wastepaper baskets, etc.

❀

Stitch pennants on solid-colored felt or other material to make an attractive bedspread for a child or teen-ager.

❀

Make delightful, inexpensive curtains for a child's bedroom: Have the child crayon designs on muslin;

cover the muslin with wax paper and lay a cloth on top; press with a warm iron until the designs are fixed on the fabric.

❀

Keep a child's sandbox clean, dry and pet-proof by making a cover out of a plastic tablecloth. Simply hem the tablecloth on a sewing machine, insert elastic into the hem and gather the edge to fit.

❀

Make a child's crayon drawings into place mats: Put a drawing face up on the ironing board (put newspapers under the drawing to protect the ironing board cover); cover the drawing with a 12″ x 17″ piece of cotton sheeting; iron the fabric firmly at a low to medium setting until the drawing is transferred to the fabric. Let the fabric cool. Seal the fabric between two layers of clear adhesive paper.

❀

To make an extra special, as well as practical, teddy bear, try this: Make the bear out of fake fur; insert a zipper in one seam; put a hot water bottle inside. The neck of the bottle fits into the bear's head.

❀

Make a lamp from a large bleach or detergent jug. Buy an adjustable socket from a hardware or dime store; pierce the side of the jug near the bottom for the wire to pass through. Weigh down with pennies.

❀

Use colored fruit, large roses or flower bouquets cut from an oilcloth pattern to decorate cupboards, etc.

Cut designs carefully with small scissors and adhere them with wallpaper paste; they stay firmly attached and the waxy surface is easy to wipe clean.

❀

Use old percolator stems, painted in bright enamel colors, as single candle holders for tiny Danish tapers.

❀

Toilet paper makes a good substitute for Japanese rice paper when decorating on glass. Spray glue on the glass and press on a single thickness of toilet paper. Do not try to smooth—the wrinkles make the interesting effect. Cut enough tissues to patch along edges; the joinings will not show.

❀

Put inexpensive clear glass bowls, vases or glasses in a shallow box filled with white sand and place in the sun. After a few months, the glass will be permanently tinted a myriad of beautiful colors. The longer the sunning, the deeper the shade.

❀

Make colorful snakes from neckties for a gift that delights children of all ages. Stuff ties with old stockings. Stitch across both ends. Add buttons for eyes; embroider a nose and eyelashes; for fangs, attach a long, forked strip of red felt under the necktie's wide end.

❀

Spray glue on an old picture frame and sprinkle aquarium rocks or small shells evenly on the frame. When dry, shake the frame; spray glue again and fill in the bare spots. Repeat the process until the frame is completely covered.

❀

Make an original dressing-table tray that will bring back pleasant memories: Insert a favorite snapshot into an inexpensive picture frame, glue a piece of blotter to the back and paint the frame to match your bedroom.

❀

When picture-hanging space is limited, make a "gallery"—which can also serve as a room divider— from a louvered door, or shutters joined together. Paint to match room decor, or leave a natural wood color. Attach pictures and other objects by looping picture wire around the louvers.

❀

If draperies are too expensive, use neutral-colored material, such as muslin. Later, use the muslin to line the more expensive draperies.

❀

Brighten a dark room by hanging yellow curtains over windows.

❀

Make exquisite curtains out of kitchen towels that have lively designs and perky colors.

8.

For Special
Occasions

Baby Showers and New Arrivals

Wrap a gift for a new baby in the front page of the newspaper printed on the day the child was born; also include the horoscope, the weather report and the "personals" column.

❀

Make a coin collection for a new baby, saving coins from the year in which he was born.

❀

Give a father-to-be a surprise baby shower.

❀

Give the father-to-be a waiting-room present: a box containing dimes, magazines, cigarettes, gum, candy and telephone numbers.

❀

Give a "grandparents" shower for those expecting their first grandchild. Gifts should be all the things needed when the new baby comes to visit—baby spoons and dishes, bibs, teething rings, rattles and other toys.

❀

When a close friend who has moved away is expecting a baby, have a shower *in absentia.* Have guests bring their gifts to the party unwrapped; serve refreshments; wrap the presents together and put them in a box for mailing.

❀

To be sure new mothers do not get "lost in the shuffle" after having a baby, and to show special love and pride for her part in the event, give her personal gifts for her own use rather than for the new baby.

❀

Cut a watermelon in the shape of a cradle for the centerpiece at a summer baby shower. Cut the watermelon meat into cubes; add other fruit—cantaloupe cubes, grapes, slices of peaches—and add a little lemonade to give tang and to help the fruit retain its color.

❀

Help a child adjust to a new baby in the family by giving him or her a surprise baby-doll shower, modeled on those given to the mother.

❀

Inexperienced new mothers will feel more confident about giving infants a bath with this unusual gift: thin cotton gloves. They assure a firm grip on wiggly children in the tub, and enable the free hand to be used as a washcloth. Rinse out gloves after bath time and hang them to dry, ready for use the next morning.

❀

Make stork favors for baby showers: Open a two-inch safety pin; bend back the side with the clasp. Break a colored toothpick in two; push broken end into pin clasp. Bend the other side of the pin into a right angle and stick it into a gumdrop. Tie a tiny bow around the stork's neck.

Birthdays

On birthdays, in addition to the traditional gifts, plan small ways of showing love. Each family member can do a chore on the sly that is normally the duty of the honoree.

❀

Write down whims expressed by friends or loved ones during the year. On birthdays, or on other special occasions, indulge them with a horseback ride, theater tickets, yoga lessons, etc.

❀

Make an exciting, inexpensive birthday gift for a small child: Cover a box with wrapping paper; cut a slot in the top. Tape pennies every few inches along a strand of ribbon; put the ribbon in the box and pull one end through the slot. Tape the box shut. As the child pulls the ribbon, he will have the excitement of finding penny after penny, cutting them off, and dreaming of what to do with his new-found treasure.

❀

Grandparents with limited funds and many grandchildren can use this birthday gift idea. Save pennies in a big coffee can and let the birthday child grab as many as his hand will hold.

❀

When grandparents live far away, help your children feel closer to them by celebrating their birthdays as though they were there. Set a festive table, complete with cake and candles; sing "Happy Birthday"; have the children make wishes for the grandparents before blowing out the candles.

❀

Children born near Christmas often feel cheated, so let them celebrate their birthdays on another day—such as the Fourth of July—or share the birthday of a beloved relative.

❀

A miniature aquarium is an inexpensive, quickly made birthday gift for a child who has a large collection of fish. Put sand, stones, a snail, a couple of baby guppies and a small piece of tank greenery in a baby-food jar. Cover. Tape a card and bow to the top. At the party, the children can watch as the new fish are transferred to the main tank.

❀

Send a child's birthday party invitations on balloons. Inflate the balloons; write the date, time and place of the party on them; deflate and mail.

❀

Instead of place cards for a child's birthday party, blow up balloons and with a felt-tip pen write the guests' names on them. Tie the balloons to the backs of chairs.

❀

For a child's birthday party, make edible name cards from cookies; write guests' names with icing.

❀

The night before a birthday party, fill cupcake papers with ice cream, make faces on them with small candies, and place them on a tray in the freezer. After the cake has been cut, bring out the ice cream. Children will be pleased with their own individual ice cream cups and serving the ice cream will be a much neater job than usual.

❀

For inexpensive birthday party favors, buy flats of miniature marigolds; cut each section apart, and wrap in colorful paper.

❀

Use round candies with holes in the centers as candle holders for children's birthday cakes.

❀

Make unusual birthday party hats as follows. Buy balloons and heavy construction paper. Staple ends of paper strips—about 22" long and 1½" wide—to make headbands. Then stretch another strip about 6" long across the top and staple it to the band. Punch a hole in the center of the top band and insert the knotted end of an inflated balloon.

❀

Ask guests at a child's birthday party to autograph the tablecloth (with names and date). Embroider each entry. Use the cloth each year, adding new names, repeating old ones.

❀

Have a tearless birthday party for toddlers by giving everyone a gift. Instead of taking presents to the honoree, ask mothers to bring one item suitable for a grab bag. Let all the children go home with a present.

❀

Instead of a traditional party, take your child and a small group of his best friends on a train ride to a nearby town. Spend the day sightseeing before boarding the train for the trip home. Many children today have never been on a train; it will be a day for them to remember.

❀

Celebrate a child's birthday with a "cook-it-yourself" luncheon. Let the guests and honoree make the meal and set the table just as they desire.

❀

Children under five can share more fully in each other's birthdays if allowed to frost the cake. Mix vanilla frosting in small bowls with various food colorings and let each sibling help draw a picture on the cake, with frosting. This is a great tradition year after year and a way for children to gain a sense of pride about sharing.

Bridal Showers, Weddings and Anniversaries

When sending shower invitations, enclose two file cards marked "My Favorite Recipe" and "My Recipe for a Happy Marriage." Ask each guest to mail back the filled-out cards. Put the cards in a file box and present it as your hostess gift to the bride.

❀

Have bridal shower guests sign a guest book and include their telephone numbers and addresses. Present this as your hostess gift to the bride. She will have all the information necessary for writing her thank-yous.

❀

For a wedding shower, make a starter recipe book from a three-ring binder. Decorate the cover with the bride's new name; fill some of the pages with your favorite recipes, nutrition charts, freezing guides, herb charts, measuring equivalents and cooking tips. Spray the cover and the pages on which you have written with clear plastic spray, so that they can be wiped clean with a sponge.

❀

Rags make an unusual gift for a linen shower, and can be given alone or in addition to new linens. Clean and press rags; pink the edges; attach a label to each, giving its purpose—a lint-free rag for window polishing, flannel pieces for silver polishing, etc.

❀

For an unusual bridal shower gift, give a claw hammer, pliers, small and medium Phillips screwdrivers, small and medium flathead screwdrivers, a tape measure and small nails.

❀

For a bridal shower gift, select a theme, such as dishwashing, and give a dishpan, dishcloth, soap, cleanser, rubber scraper and scouring pads—all the utensils necessary for completing a single job.

❀

In addition to one new gift, ask bridal shower guests to offer one item from their own household goods that they no longer need to use, or a duplicate of an item in their possession. This is especially a nice idea for a bride who is only being given one shower in her honor.

❀

Close relatives or friends of a bride-to-be can give an unusual party that will help them get acquainted with the groom: Give a "his" shower and brunch, with appropriate gifts—tools, camping equipment, etc.

❀

When an invalid relative or close family friend will not be able to attend your wedding, take part of the wedding to her: Have the final fitting of the wedding dress in her home. Even at a nursing home there is room for a "fitting party."

❀

Give a sapling for a wedding present and it will be treasured for years to come.

❀

A family member of a bride- or groom-to-be can give the lovely, practical gift of a notebook filled with the names and addresses of the new wife's or husband's relatives. Other facts, such as special interests, birthdays, ages of children, can be noted alongside each name. This helps acquaint the newlyweds with each other's families and is also a great help when it is time to write thank-you notes.

❀

Give a thoughtful and economical wedding present: Take candid snapshots the day of the wedding, the kind professional photographers would overlook. Put them in a photo album and present it to the couple after they return from their honeymoon.

❀

Retrieve champagne bottles from a wedding reception. The next Christmas or on the first wedding anniversary, present the couple with a set of drinking glasses cut from the bottles.

❀

Root sprigs from a bridal bouquet or wedding decorations and present them as plants to newlyweds on their first anniversary.

❀

Give your hobbyist spouse a room of his or her own for an anniversary present: Clean out the attic, or a space in the garage that has been used to store junk.

❀

When choosing a gift for a newly married friend, remember that personal luxuries such as perfume, lingerie, etc., can often lift spirits much more than practical items like pillowcases, dish towels or kitchenware.

Christmas, Holidays and Holiday Gift-Giving

Have children make their own Christmas cards by tracing the outline of their hands on red or green construction paper; cut the hands out; decorate with seals and greetings.

❊

Share the beauty of your garden with friends all year around by enclosing little packets of seeds, gathered in the fall from your choice flowers, in greeting cards. Divide seeds into numerous waxed-paper sandwich bags; label and seal with tiny flower stickers.

❊

Use Christmas cards to decorate big boxes that are awkward and expensive to wrap. Cut the illustrations off cards and glue to boxes. Selecting colors and scenes to go side by side is as creative as making a patchwork quilt.

❊

Children can make creative, inexpensive Christmas gift tags with a box of assorted cookie cutters (bells, stars, gingerbread men, Christmas trees, etc.), used greeting cards, pencils, scissors, a hole puncher and a ball of red or green twine. Place cookie cutter over the Christmas card, outline with pencil, cut out, punch a hole at one end, insert colored string and there you have it!

Make a Christmas wreath of eight played-out tennis balls. Dye balls bright red or green; let them dry; then drill holes the size of a coat-hanger wire through each ball. Bend a hanger into a circle and string balls onto it. Fill in the spaces with greenery. Tie a bow at the top.

Make an Advent calendar: Cut a large piece of cardboard into the shape of a Christmas tree; glue twenty-four small foil tins to the tree. Inside each put a verse, a message from an old Christmas card, a scripture verse, a trinket or candy. To conceal each day's surprise, cut circles of bright paper; number them 1 to 24, and glue one on top of each tin.

Make a bow tree. Pin bows and other gift package decorations to a styrofoam cone. During the Christmas season, the tree becomes a lovely table decoration; during the rest of the year, it is a handy way of storing bows for reuse.

Make Christmas tree decorations from empty thread spools. Spray them with glue; sprinkle with glitter, sequins, tiny seed pearls. Loop string through the center hole to attach to tree.

To keep it from drying out and become a fire hazard, water a Christmas tree by putting ice cubes in the base of the stand.

❋

Wire twisters used to fasten bread wrappers are excellent for fastening lights to Christmas trees.

❋

For those who live in nursing homes, make a Christmas tree that requires little space: Cut a piece of bright green felt into the shape of a tree; glue it to a sheet of cardboard; decorate with glitter, sequins, beads and old costume jewelry. Provide a loop at the top for hanging.

❋

Let each child pick out one new tree ornament every Christmas. When storing the ornaments after the holidays, put each child's ornaments into his own box. When the children are ready to leave home, they will have a treasured collection ready for their own trees.

❋

To make a tasty Christmas tree ornament or gift for holiday callers, wrap small pieces of fruitcake in transparent, colored tissue paper or kitchen cellophane and tie with odds and ends of colored yarn.

❋

Take color photographs of a friend's flowerbeds in bloom; mount them in a small album and give the photo collection as a gift at Christmas.

❋

Enclose a favorite recipe with homemade Christmas gifts, choosing a recipe that complements the gift—a bread recipe with homemade jam, for example.

❀

Elderly people can pay back the kindliness of young neighbors with children by enclosing a note in Christmas cards offering to babysit for each couple several times during the coming year.

❀

Include a package of thank-you notes in children's Christmas stockings, to be used after presents are opened.

Easter

Children can join in preparing these Easter gifts: At the beginning of Lent, sow flower seeds in pots. A few days before Easter decorate the pots with strips of contact paper; cut Easter Bunny name tags from construction paper, clearly marking each recipient's name on the ears; tape the bunny to a pipe cleaner and insert it in pot.

❀

About six weeks before Easter begin blowing out all eggs used in cooking. When Easter arrives, there will be plenty of eggs to decorate without the usual problem of what to do with too many hard-boiled eggs.

❀

A few weeks before Easter, to save time and avoid discoloring cups and bowls, put aside small, empty cans which can be used to hold Easter egg dye and then discarded.

❊

Onion skins placed in boiling water will dye Easter eggs all shades from dark maroon to light orange, depending on the amount of skins used.

❊

Bake special cookies at Eastertime: Cut out a cardboard pattern of an egg, lay it down over rolled-out cookie dough and cut around it with a sharp knife. Sprinkle the entire batch of eggs with colored sugar and bake to a very light brown. The end results look like real eggs, speckled by the Easter Bunny.

Halloween

Take photographs of trick-or-treaters. Give each child a treat in a bag stapled to a note telling when to return for the photograph.

❊

Use contact paper to make "masks" for parties and at Halloween. Cut paper into strips for Indian warpaint; or cut out eyebrows, warts, circles and other odd shapes. Let the children decorate themselves.

General Hints for Parties and Gift-Giving, Decorating and Gift Wrapping

General Hints

For a housewarming, try an old-fashioned "pounding" party: Have each guest bring one pound of a staple.

❀

Set up a community borrowing system for cups, saucers, casseroles and other serving items for special occasions and parties. Get together and draw up a list of items, by category and by name of the supplier, that each person is willing to lend. Circulate copies of the list to keep on hand for reference. Ground rules: The borrower must take the responsibility to clean, return or promptly replace each item. And no one is obligated to invite the lender to the party! This works wonders for those who live in limited spaces—trailer homes, for example—or for those with limited budgets.

❀

As a unique gift for ecologically minded new homeowners, give a collection of plants that provide food and shelter for birds and wildlife.

❀

For a travel gift, give a real "nest egg" by punching a small hole in one end of an egg; emptying and washing it; and forcing a bill through the hole. Place the egg on cellophane grass.

❀

When a soon-to-be traveler asks your favorite color to help in choosing a gift abroad, give the traveler a spool of thread—it is easy to pack and eliminates the guesswork in choosing the right shade.

❀

Give a college-bound student a small electric coffee-pot or an inexpensive heating element, with a large mug and a selection of instant coffee, cocoa, tea bags and instant soups. This gift will be greatly appreciated on those first, rushed mornings and during all-night studying sessions.

❀

Give a college-bound student a snack kit: Wrap up a can opener; a red-handled knife, fork and spoon; a cloth napkin and a red plastic cup, all in a brightly colored checked dish towel.

❀

Tuck a few dustrags into a college-bound suitcase —a greatly appreciated "gift" for dorm use.

❀

For birthdays, anniversaries and Christmas, elderly people can give many of their own keepsakes of a life-time—family treasures are special gifts that almost everyone appreciates.

Decorating

Insert tiny straw flowers in empty spools of thread for shower or luncheon table decorations.

❀

Melt tag ends of soap and pour into small, greased gelatin molds: Use appropriate molds to make party favors or shower, Christmas or children's birthday gifts.

❀

Make a festive centerpiece by sticking cut flowers between the leaves of a pineapple top. Put the top in a bowl of water; set on a platter. Arrange cut pineapple around the base of the bowl.

❀

Fuchsia blossoms, placed on a frosted cake, make beautiful birthday candle holders.

Gift Wrapping

When wrapping gifts, make an unusual, inexpensive package by painting on colorful "ribbons" with felt-tip pens or grease pencils.

❀

Wrap a gift in a bandanna and tie it up hobo style.

❀

Wrap unwieldly items in a custom-made paper or cloth bag, using an ordinary paper bag as a pattern. Punch holes near the top, two inches apart; string a ribbon through; gather and tie the ribbon into a bow.

❀

Use children's artwork to wrap presents—especially those for grandparents and others close to the children.

❀

Enclose with thank-you notes a snapshot showing the gift being used or displayed.

9.

Travel Tips

Motor Trips and Car Hints

Before long motor trips, fasten a shoe bag to the back of the front set for a handy storage area. Maps, postcards, tourist information and other items will be organized and available.

❀

When traveling, if space inside the car is limited, button hanger clothing inside a raincoat or cover the items with a plastic bag and lay them on top of the luggage in the trunk. The clothes will arrive clean and wrinkle-free.

❀

For those who suffer from cold feet while traveling or sitting at home, set your feet in a large grocery bag and pull the bag up to the knees. Paper is a good insulator that will prevent drafts and retain heat.

❀

Before traveling—whether off to college or to Europe—fill a plastic lidded freezer container with toiletries and pack it into the suitcase.

❀

Before a trip or a picnic, chill iced tea in an open thermos overnight, in the refrigerator. It will be doubly cold the next day at lunchtime.

❀

When traveling and eating frequently in restaurants, eat the main meal at noon—many restaurants charge more for the same meals at night.

❀

Keep stale bread in a bag in the glove compartment of the car or camper: It will always be available for feeding wildlife.

❀

Store several short boards in the car trunk to insure having a firm foundation for the jack, if needed.

❀

When appliances are located in the back of the garage and you need help in judging the distance while parking the car, tie a fishing bobber to a string and hang it from the rafters. When the bobber touches the windshield, you will know you have reached the proper stopping point.

❀

Women who drive a car frequently can lengthen the life of good dress shoes by keeping a pair of old shoes in the car for use while driving.

❀

Net scrubbers for pots and pans are good "bug removers" for windshields.

Camping and Cooking at the Campsite

Camping

For privacy at night when camping out in the station wagon, spread a sudsy glass cleaner over windows. In the morning, wipe with a paper towel.

❀

To provide ice and beverages while camping or on a boating trip, freeze water, lemonade, tea, etc., in gallon-size plastic milk jugs and store on board in portable ice chests. The frozen liquids will keep other items in the chest cold, will melt slowly to provide icy drinks from time to time, and will prevent everything from floating in water. One jug will stay cold up to a day and a half.

❀

Fit the bottom of a fishing tackle box with styrofoam. Stick hooks, flies and plugs into the foam; they will stay clean and handy, and fingers will not be cut by hooks. Should the box overturn in water, the foam block will float and can be retrieved easily.

❀

Give yourself a private dressing room for camping trips. Take along a hula hoop, a shower curtain and shower curtain hooks. Hang the curtain to the hoop and suspend it from a branch of a nearby tree.

❀

If standard ice blocks are too large for your camper's ice box, buy a plastic container the same size as the ice tray; before each trip, fill the container and freeze.

❀

Keep a complete record of camping trips by listing your campsites on your tent with a felt-tip marker. It's a real conversation-starter.

❀

To prevent clothes from becoming damp when camping, keep each outfit in a separate plastic bag. Roll the garments tightly to prevent wrinkles. Use duffel bags instead of suitcases, for they are more easily stuffed into odd corners in the car.

❀

When camping, heat water for dishes by filling four large cans with water and using them to support the campfire grill.

❀

When traveling or camping in extremely hot climates, keep aerosol cans from exploding by putting them in the camper refrigerator or ice chest.

❀

When camping or picnicking, mix all condiments used on hot dogs or hamburgers and put them in one jar. This makes a good relish and eliminates excess baggage.

Cooking at the Campsite

"Steam" grease and food off a barbecue grill: When the grill is removed from the fire, wrap it immediately in several thicknesses of wet newspapers. Steam forming under the papers will loosen the grease and carbon build-up, which will then fall off under hot running water.

❀

Use coffee tins to "bake" an easy outdoor meal: Layer very thin pork chops alternately with carrots, onions, sliced potatoes, green peppers and green peas. Salt, pepper, and dot each layer with butter. Cover the can with two thicknesses of foil. Bury the cans in a bed of hot coals. After a half hour or so, the dinner-in-a-can will be ready. For variety, try sweet potatoes accompanied by sliced apples and/or oranges with brown sugar—or veal or chicken can be used instead of pork.

❀

When starting charcoal, pile briquettes in a pyramid; the fire will build more quickly.

❀

When cooking with charcoal, put foods on that will be eaten another day; freeze and reheat when ready to use. This saves on charcoal.

❀

Make long-lasting ice cylinders for wide-mouthed thermos bottles by freezing water in frozen-orange-juice cans.

❄

Cut the legs of an old card table down to about six inches to make a low table for camping out or picnicking at the beach.

❄

Eliminate the mess of buttering corn on the cob at cookouts: Fill a large quart jar with hot water and add two sticks of butter. When the butter melts, put a cob in the jar and pull it out slowly. The butter, which floats on the top of the water, coats the corn perfectly.

Traveling with Children

When planning a family trip, get children involved by sending travel information requests in their names.

❄

Pack a child's favorite stuffed animals into a tote bag before a long trip: Familiar personal belongings give reassurance in new, unfamiliar surroundings.

❄

When traveling great distances with small children, pin labels with vital information into their pockets. When traveling by air, include the name of the airline and flight number; on trips overseas, also include their passport numbers.

❄

Before traveling long distances with children, put drinks in well-washed detergent bottles—the kind with snip-off tops; mark the bottles with each child's name and freeze them. The bottles will prevent spillage and the drinks will remain cool as the ice thaws slowly during the trip.

❀

A king-size pillowcase makes a good sheet for an infant's car bed. If the child spits up, the mattress can be turned and used on the other side.

❀

When traveling with children under three, take balloons along to prevent boredom. Blow them up and let the children draw faces on them.

❀

When traveling with young children ages six to nine, help them remember details of trips by giving them pencils and pads of paper. Ask them to note the names of towns and villages you pass through, the date and time, and any impressions they felt when stopping or passing through. For example, one notation might read:

New Hebron, Mississippi
11:22 A.M., March 3
big old store on the corner
the owner let me fish pickles out of a big barrel

❀

So that children can play favorite board games during car trips, apply Velcro® to the game's playing pieces and to the playing board.

❀

Before traveling with children, pack a box with several cans of tuna, small boxes of raisins, shelled peanuts, a small jar of peanut butter, a box of dry cereal, a jar of cocoa mixed with powdered milk and sugar, a loaf of bread and a bag of oranges and apples. Include also paper plates, bowls and cups; napkins; a can opener; a sharp knife; and a bag of disposable cutlery. Children love impromptu meals in motels and they cost about a third as much as the average coffee shop meal.

❅

To prevent closing car doors on children's fingers, give them a game to play: Usher them into the car and ask, "Who can cover their ears first?" Then close the door quickly.

❅

When going to the beach with an enormous amount of gear for children, put the items—umbrellas, towels, beach balls, blankets, etc.—into a plastic sled and pull it across the sand. If there is a toddler in the family, let him ride in front.

10.

Raising Children

Family Harmony and Togetherness

Adopt an idea from the Chinese to bring harmony to a family with many children: Put the eldest "in-charge-of-the-happiness" of the next in line; the second, in turn, is in charge of the happiness of the next, and so on. The children, having such responsibility, will solve many of their difficulties among themselves.

❀

Get into the habit of complimenting your children by taking time to notice the nice things they do. Children like praise as much as parents do—you'll find that you have much less need for correcting if you use plenty of praise.

❀

Regardless of age, put one member in charge of the "worrying" for everyone, each day. The routine keeps tension low and cooperation among families at an all-time high.

❀

To help conserve energy and to give children a glimpse into what life was like before modern conveniences, have several Old Time days each year—turning down the thermostat (not so far as to risk frozen pipes); using no electricity; cooking in the fireplace; gathering together to read or swap stories in the candlelight.

❀

Give an aspiring young dancer or gymnast the joyous responsibility of becoming the family "exercise leader," demonstrating skills and helping others in the family, including mother, father, sister or brother, in weekly exercise sessions at home.

❀

To keep small children quiet and attentive during formal meetings such as church services or concerts, sit as close to the front row as possible. Being able to see—and be seen—will have a marked effect on their conduct.

❀

Remove the indefinite, frustrating "in just a minute" response to a child who interrupts chores when in need of a mother's help or companionship: Set the kitchen timer to determine a definite stopping-off place. The child will find it easier to be patient when a specific time limit has been set, and the chore will get done as the timer ticks away.

❀

Keep a "tear" bottle. When a child cries, rush for the bottle to catch the tears. Soon he will be running for the bottle himself, and in the excitement of the game, the tears will be forgotten.

❀

Make up private signals for correcting children in front of visitors. For example, like football signals, you might use numbers: Instead of saying, "Get your elbows off the table," simply say a number that means the same.

❀

When grocery shopping with a young child, allevi-
ate boredom or mischief-making by making him a
partner in your task. Give him a small list of items
with their approximate prices and enough money to
cover the cost. Let the child proceed on his own with
his own shopping basket, paying for the items at the
check-out counter and collecting his own trading
stamps.

❀

When a self-reliant toddler causes anxiety about
safety, appoint him or her the leader when crossing
the street ("You'd better take Mom's hand and lead
her across the street so she won't get hit by a car")
or when shopping in the supermarket, sending the
toddler off to locate the next item needed. The child
will enjoy feeling important, and will learn responsibility.

❀

Put a low clothesline next to the regular line and
let a young child hang up his or her own clothes.
Not only a time-saver, but also a good way to teach
shared responsibilities.

❀

During school vacations, instead of taking reluctant
children around with you while running errands, drop
them off at the children's library and specify your
time of return to them and the librarian.

❀

When a child is anxious over the arrival of a new
baby in the family, show him snapshots and home
movies made when he was an infant. He will soon

acquire a new understanding of the dependency of an infant and the stages in its development. With this understanding, his own anxieties will lessen.

❀

When an afternoon finds a new mother and her infant in tired and cranky moods, a good pick-me-up is to take a long, warm bath together. The warm water erases tension; being so close makes both feel better.

❀

On voting day, instead of calling a sitter, take your preschoolers with you. They will be fascinated by seeing the lines of grown-ups waiting in turn, hearing the names—including yours—checked against the list and seeing people disappear into the mysterious booth. You will be bombarded with questions about the strange process called "voting." Take them whenever you must vote; explain as much as they can grasp. The children will begin to understand and appreciate the value of the voting process at a very early age.

❀

When there's no time to acquaint children with a new babysitter, set up a treasure hunt before you leave. Hide about ten notes all over the house, each a question that the children must answer in order to find the next clue. For example, "Where can you find a glass, a spoon, a plate, a shoe, etc.?" At the end of the hunt, they find a special item to share with their new friend—popcorn to roast, a new coloring book, etc.—and the sitter will be accepted as a companion in joining in with the children.

❀

When children begin to complain that they are too old for babysitters, working mothers might try this solution during the summer months. Hire an "entertainment director"—a teen-ager with enough skill and interest to take the children to the city library, instructing them on its use; lead field trips; supervise experiments in crafts, cookery, literature or sewing.

❀

When a youngster refuses to wear the clothes you pick out, lay out three outfits on the bed side by side; then let the child select what to wear. Having a choice will make all the difference.

❀

When a child balks at putting away his toys, offer to do this chore in exchange for doing one of yours.

❀

When a child refuses to practice a musical instrument, share the "torture." Take turns practicing the same tunes. After the child understands that he is not alone in making mistakes, he will progress; and with progress, he will no longer need your physical presence.

❀

Instead of nagging children, try writing reminder notes on a blackboard hung in their rooms. Also use the blackboard to compliment them when tasks are done and to share thoughts that come to you when they are away at school during the day.

❀

Every few months parents can reward an older child who helps with young siblings by taking him

or her out alone with them to dinner, a movie or another special event.

❀

To make a parent–teen-ager discussion on dating,
dress or other emotionally charged issues more pro-
ductive, try having a meal together in a quiet res-
taurant and beginning the discussion over dessert.

❀

On Saturdays and holidays, make a game out of
chores by drawing lots—one slip of paper for every
family member, with a chore written on each except
for one, which says, "Relax!"

❀

When children work in the yard, give them the
same courtesy you would give someone hired to work:
Take them iced drinks for an occasional break.

❀

To cut down on television viewing, give each child
in the family a small sum over his regular allowance.
Each time he watches a program, subtract a nickel
from his bonus. The children will select their programs
more carefully.

❀

When a child is upset by a parent's out-of-town
business trips, establish a link by teaching the child
about the state or country being visited. In addition,
buy a large picture puzzle of the United States or a
map of the foreign country and let the child carry the
state or country around with him.

❀

Insure a child's happiness when moving—especially if it is to a home with smaller quarters: Give the child responsibility to choose which special belongings to take along and to put the items into a carton by himself. The carton size should match the amount of space available in the new home for the best-treasured belongings.

❀

Even the smallest child need not be excluded from receiving mail. Those too young to read will be equally delighted with a letter "written" by pictures cut from a magazine and pasted to stationery.

❀

To help children feel better acquainted with cousins who live far away, try exchanging life-size paper dolls. Have the children lie down on large sheets of brown paper; draw around the outline of their bodies. Let each child dress and color his own replica, then fold and mail the paper dolls.

Eating

When getting a baby to eat is a problem, try taping a picture of another baby to the high-chair tray. Feed each spoonful of food to the baby in the picture before offering it to the child.

❀

At baby's feeding time, wear a bib tied around the neck and turned over the "burping" shoulder to protect clothes.

❀

Make lunchtime with young schoolchildren more pleasant by reading to them as they eat.

❀

If a child insists on eating from a grown-up-size plate, use a glass pie plate.

❀

Spill-proof any dish or bowl with a suction soap holder. Dampen one side of the rubber disk holder and press it to the bottom of the dish; then press dish to high chair or table.

❀

Drinking glasses are less likely to slip from the hands if several wide rubber bands are placed around the glass.

❀

Eliminate picky eating habits by using this trick: When new food comes to the table, give it to grown-ups only, commenting that young children probably would not like it. After the children plead for a taste, appear to weaken and concede to give them just a tiny piece, commenting that they surely won't like it. The small serving will almost always "taste wonderful" even if only a common parsnip!

❀

When feeding solids to an infant or a toddler, use colored plastic spoons. There will be no more fussing or loss of appetite.

❀

Give young children crispy, crunchy frozen peas at snack time—they make much better munching than "junk" foods or sweets, particularly before dinner.

❀

Free family meals from the interruptions of neighborhood children. Paste a picture of a family eating to a cardboard and hang the sign from the front doorknob. Tell the children not to ring the doorbell until the sign comes down.

❀

Encourage children to eat gelatin-based dishes by using imaginative molds; search toy departments for heat-resistant plastic shellfish, sand castles, automobiles, etc.

❀

When children resist sitting down for a proper lunch, insure that they eat properly by giving them ice cream cones filled with tuna or egg salad, cottage cheese or yogurt.

Sleeping

While working in the kitchen, keep a baby content by placing the child—strapped into an infant seat—on top of the dishwasher or washing machine. The gentle vibration will lull the baby to sleep, leaving you free to work in the room—and the child will always be in sight.

❀

To keep an infant covered during the night, fix the blanket as follows: Stitch a piece of old sheeting— the same length as the blanket and the same width as the mattress—to the sides of the blanket. Place the sheeting under the mattress; fold the blanket over the baby and tuck in.

❀

When a child has trouble sleeping, focus his attention on something else: Dab a generous amount of cologne to the back of his hand and tell him to sniff it till the scent is gone. The deep breathing and concentration will send him off to sleep in no time.

❀

To make nap times more appealing, play soothing music or children's stories on a record player.

❀

Parents of small children can protect their "extra forty winks" on Saturday mornings by leaving a surprise bag by children's beds. In the bag put things that children can create with—glue, bits of fabric, paper, crayons, pipe cleaners, etc. Vary the items each week.

❀

Give the child who sleeps on the bottom half of a bunk bed something to look at by putting an old fitted sheet over the mattress bottom on the top bunk. Let the "bottom bunker" decorate his "ceiling" with a felt-tip pen.

Bathing, Grooming and Dressing

Put "daisy" footholds in a baby's plastic bathtub to prevent slipping and to keep him occupied during baths.

❀

Give a young child a rubber doll and washrag at bathtime: Your toddler will bathe his or her child, while you bathe yours.

❀

Toddlers fussy about taking baths can be amused by spraying shaving cream into their hands and adding a few drops of food coloring. They will forget their displeasure as they "paint" themselves and the bathtub walls.

❀

A child will wash his face with greater success if a mirror is hung at his eye level in the bathroom.

❀

Encourage daily tooth care by young children: Hang a monthly calendar in the bathroom and hand out colored stars (one color per child) for each day when they've brushed morning and evening. Give a small bonus gift to the child with the most stars at the end of each month.

❀

Give a child who resists grooming a "hygiene kit." Buy an inexpensive plastic carrying case; print his name on the outside; fill with travel-size tubes of toothpaste, cakes of soap, a toothbrush, a comb, etc.

❀

At hair-washing time, keep shampoo out of children's eyes by giving them underwater goggles to wear.

❀

Try this hair-grooming trick for black children: After washing, rolling or plaiting hair, put a stocking cap over the child's head. (One leg of an old pair of pantyhose makes a good cap.) The cap will keep the hairdo in place overnight and will also absorb excess oil.

❀

To cut a squirmy child's bangs evenly, put a piece of transparent tape across the bangs and cut above the tape.

❀

When hair is thin, stick moleskin on the backs of barrettes to hold them in place.

❀

Hang a mirror behind a baby's changing table. The child will enjoy watching himself in the mirror and changing will be easier.

❀

To keep a baby quiet during diaper changes, staple a picture of his favorite thing—a dog, for instance—to the ceiling above the changing table.

❀

Prevent babies from unwinding the toilet paper while they're being toilet trained by keeping a rubber band around the toilet paper roller. When the baby is on the toilet, slip the rubber band over the toilet paper.

❀

When children have a difficult time keeping on their slippers, sew into each slipper the elastic knitted top of an old sock.

❀

To prevent a toddler's tripping over shoelaces, re-lace with ⅛″ elastic; do not stretch while lacing. Tie the excess elastic in a knot. This eliminates dangling shoelaces, and also allows the child to put shoes on and take them off by himself.

❀

To keep children's feet extra warm and dry in the winter, cover socks and shoes with a pair of large, heavy woolen socks before slipping on fairly loose galoshes.

❀

Help a child to zip galoshes by fastening a small notebook ring in the zipper pull of each. Galoshes can be hooked together by the rings when put in the school or home closet.

❀

Forgetting sweaters at school during cold weather can be prevented by sewing an old sweater right into a child's coat.

❀

Mittens crocheted right onto the sleeves of a child's old sweater will never get lost.

❀

To help an older child break the habit of fingernail biting, suggest that he or she stop the habit one finger at a time—the nicer appearance of one nail will be encouragement to try with another.

Child Safety

Provide a toddler with an obvious identification tag for family vacation or shopping trips. Buy a stainless steel dog tag; have it stamped with the child's name, address and telephone number. String the tag on the bottom lace of the child's shoe.

❀

For keeping an eye on children in a crowded swimming pool, paint the children's names in bright nail polish on the top of their bathing caps.

❀

As precious time is often lost trying to identify those injured in an accident, glue an identification card with name, address and phone number to the handlebars of all bicycles in the household.

❀

For ease in keeping an eye on a toddler while shopping, tie a helium-filled balloon to his arm; should he wander, he can easily be spotted.

❀

Teach small children to raise their hands when crossing streets. This makes them appear "taller" and therefore more visible to motorists.

❀

Children who recognize numbers but do not yet read should have their own emergency "telephone directory." Next to the telephone, place a card with numbers—such as those of the fire department, police department, grandparents, parents' office numbers, etc.—and draw an appropriate face to correspond to each number.

❀

As a safety precaution for dark, rainy days, put reflector tape on the heels and toes of rain boots.

❀

To keep track of a toddler at home, tie a small bell to his or her shoe.

❀

Make a "speaking tube" for calling children by extending a length of garden hose from the kitchen door to the children's playhouse.

Schoolwork, Learning and the Value of Money

Schoolwork and Learning

When children are habitually late for school, make a new policy: Instead of nagging them to "hurry," "make your bed," or "drink your milk," say nothing —only announce the departure time when it arrives. The children will soon accept their own responsibilities.

❀

Children who balk at the work of improving reading, arithmetic and fractions will tackle the problems quickly and cheerfully if taught to cook and bake following the measurements in the recipes.

❀

A child who has trouble paying attention to detail in his schoolwork can be helped by means of a hobby. Nature studies, such as bird watching, are good for developing an eye for detail which will soon carry over into schoolwork.

❀

Help a child with learning problems feel recognized and appreciated by having an "at-home honor roll." Attach several long strips of heavy material, about three inches wide, to your kitchen door and pin up pictures, arithmetic tests and spelling lessons every week.

❀

To improve a child's reading, help him write and illustrate his own book. Take snapshots of friends and family members in various activities. Have the child tell a short story about each picture. Type the stories, mount them with the photos on construction paper and staple the pages together into a "book." Reading his own stories, he will read the sentences thought for thought, rather than word for word. For spelling and punctuation improvement, have him copy the story. For variety, take another roll of film and begin another book.

❀

A child who needs reading improvement will benefit greatly from receiving mail. Even working mothers and fathers can take a few seconds out of each day to jot down and mail a quick note. The child will be eager to read his mail as soon as he comes home from school.

❀

Encourage young children to read, and to be responsible about caring for books, by helping them set up their own lending library. Make a card catalogue and number each book. Put a pocket on the back flap of each, and make a card for each. Loan time: one week. This is a great project for children in neighborhoods where they can walk from house to house.

❀

In the evening when children are doing homework, sit down and do your own "homework"—letter writing, working on the budget, paying bills, sorting through scraps of important information or memorabilia. Children will concentrate better when they feel parents are also obliged to do homework, and you will be there if needed to answer questions.

❀

A package of alphabet noodles can give children many hours of fun and help with learning words. Noodles can be glued to popsicle sticks for name pins; to paper for greeting cards; to wood for wall plaques. Alphabet noodles can also be used in spelling games. Since they are edible, they are safe for children of all ages.

❀

Teach a child the ABCs with pretzel sticks. The sticks make large letters and can be eaten as a reward when the lessons are over.

❀

Help a child with the alphabet and at the same time provide hours of play by labeling drawers of an inexpensive plastic or metal hardware cabinet and giving it as a present.

❀

To help a toddler learn numbers, make a game of climbing stairs: Cut numbers from heavy paper and tape them down in sequence to the top surface of each stair. Encourage the toddler to climb up and sit on the "age" of the child's brother, sister or neighborhood friends. The many trips up and down work off energy, an added dividend on rainy days.

❀

As soon as a child is able to talk, begin a diary. Every day set aside a few moments for the child to tell you what has happened to him or her that day. Write it down and let the child illustrate days on which something very meaningful has happened. Then, as part of the bedtime story hour, let the child choose an earlier day from the diary to be read aloud. The child will soon have the pages memorized and will begin to recognize the link between sounds and words. And most precious of all, he will have a priceless peek into his first years of life when he is older.

❀

Shaking hands with a child when he leaves for school each day will quickly teach him to distinguish between the right and left hand.

❀

Teach a youngster how to tie shoes in this easy way: Take a one-pound coffee can with a plastic snap-on top and punch two holes in the plastic about 2½" apart. Using a 24" shoelace, tie a large knot in the center so it cannot pull out, then run it through the holes from the bottom side. Snap on the top, ready for use. When it is a game rather than a job, it is possible to teach a child how to tie laces in two sessions.

❀

Save a few seeds from this year's Halloween pumpkin, dry them and keep them until spring for the children to plant. This simple lesson in plant reproduction helps teach about the continuity of life, and it's fun to think of this year's jack-o'-lantern as the offspring of the one from the year before.

The Value of Money

Make homemade coupons redeemable for cash as a present for young children. Using an unthreaded sewing machine, perforate a grid of squares on a piece of paper. In the first column write the months of the year; going across, write the dates of each Saturday in that month. On the card accompanying the coupons, explain that each square is redeemable for ten cents on the Saturday when the money is due, or at a later date.

❀

Teach young children the value of saving by setting up an allowance-interest plan. The child who waits four weeks before drawing his weekly allowance receives an extra week's allowance.

❀

In households where children are given extra money for chores, save end-of-the-week reckoning problems while teaching children how checkbooks work. Provide each child with a small notebook as a "checkbook." On the first page write "balance on hand." Newly earned money or allowances should be added to the balance on the date received. Each time the child asks for chore money, have him write a "check" on a slip of paper to turn over to the parent "banker" for cashing. Have the child deduct the amount of the check from the balance in the notebook.

❀

As each child in the family reaches the junior year of high school, put him in charge of the family checkbook—opening bills, writing checks (except the signatures), mailing deposits, keeping the balance up to date and balancing the checkbook with the bank statement. As family bookkeeper, give him a small "salary." When he leaves home—for college or a job —he will be able to manage his own expenses.

❀

Older children and teen-agers who squander money might benefit from this tip: Hold a family conference to decide on a future activity the children have always wanted to do—perhaps taking a trip to a distant city. Consent to go with the understanding that each child must pay his own way. Provided with such an incentive, budgeting and willpower come easily.

Encouraging Play

A card table draped with an old sheet makes a practical children's playhouse that can be put up and taken down in seconds. Cut windows and doorways and let the children decorate the sheet—drawing flowers, shutters, etc., with felt-tip pens.

❀

Save large cardboard appliance containers for children to make into playhouses. They can cut windows and doors and cover windows with "panes" of colored acetate. The children can decorate the inside as well as the outside of the house with marking pens or poster paints, or by gluing magazine pictures, post-cards and posters to the walls.

❊

Give a child a never-never land in one corner of his own backyard by planting a patch of winter wheat in the fall, and scattering sunflower seeds in the area in the spring. The wheat and giant sunflowers will offer the best kind of playground a child can have—an ever-changing landscape for playing anything from "house" to cowboys and Indians.

❊

Give small children a substitute "sandbox" for cold or rainy days: A shallow box filled with aquarium gravel makes a good roadbed for small cars and trucks.

❊

Encourage imaginative play by giving empty half-gallon milk cartons to children. Like building blocks, cartons can be combined in a multitude of ways, to build anything from battleships that really float to a backstop for a dart board.

❊

To prevent toy-chest lids from banging on children's fingers, stick a small suction cup on the edge of the lid; drive a nail through the cup to keep it securely in place.

❊

Avoid being confronted with the "it's mine!" battle: Clearly mark each child's name on toys with bright, shiny red nail polish.

❀

When a toddler has trouble holding on to the plastic strings of pull toys, tie screw-on tops from baby bottles to the strings. The tops are the perfect size for a small child's hand.

❀

When picture puzzles have lost their appeal, instead of buying replacements, help children create their own. Choose a picture from a magazine, paste it to cardboard and cut it into puzzle pieces.

❀

When models and toy trucks and cars break, take them apart and save the pieces in a large box. Using modeling glue, children can create fantasy vehicles out of the parts—a great pastime for a rainy day.

❀

When the boxes of much-loved games and puzzles begin to show wear, glue strips of muslin over the corners of the boxes before they break. This will help prevent losing pieces and will give the game a longer life.

❀

When a plastic swimming pool will no longer hold water above ground, sink it into the ground. Anchor it with a heavy flat stone and some sand.

Art

Give a very young child a pastry brush for water coloring: The wider handle will be easier for him to hold; the brush, which is not as flexible as a regular artist's brush, will cut down splatters; and the larger bristles will allow the child to pick up more paint.

❀

To economize on brushes for children's art projects, use pipe cleaners. Twist each end into a loop so that one pipe cleaner can be used for poster paints, water colors, gilt, enamel—any projects that do not require fine line work.

❀

Give a young artist the cap of an aerosol can as a container for rinsing his watercolor brushes. The cap's broad base makes it spill-proof.

❀

Let children draw designs with crayons on white window shades to add a gay touch to windows.

❀

Give a child a place to scribble by painting a black-board on one wall of his bedroom. Use flat black or dark blue-green latex.

❀

Let children create a mural for their playroom. Buy a large length of canvas at an art supplies store. Provide brushes, old squeeze bottles, sponges cut into smaller shapes and several small cans of brightly colored house paint. Use the driveway or garage floor for painting the mural.

❀

Plain oilcloth, thumbtacked to walls, makes an attractive, practical wall covering for a child's bedroom. It can be used as a blackboard and wiped clean; it can be replaced easily when it begins to look worn.

❀

For winter fun, make an art gallery in the yard: Press water color paintings face down in the snow. The designs will be transferred to the snow.

Toys to Make

Make a safe, simple toy for a baby by stitching a bag and stuffing it with cellophane; sew the last seam by hand so that the cellophane can be removed at laundry time. The child will enjoy the crackling sound the bag makes.

❀

To make blocks for a baby, cut the bottoms off milk cartons. Fit two same-size bottoms together; cover with self-adhesive vinyl. The blocks are easy to clean and can be tossed around without fear of damage to children or furniture.

❀

Make an inexpensive "bead kit" for small children. Save plastic straws from drive-ins and restaurants; snip straws into "beads." Make a "needle" for stringing beads by wrapping one end of a piece of yarn with cellophane tape; knot one of the beads at the other end of the yarn to keep the rest of them from falling off.

❁

Discourage young children from playing in parents' jewelry boxes by providing them with their own. Make jewelry boxes out of egg cartons, which can be spray painted or decorated with decals, and put in some of your own jewelry that you no longer wear.

❁

Make an embroidery kit for a child: Draw a simple picture on a paper plate; punch holes through the design; add a blunt needle threaded with embroidery floss.

❁

For rainy-day fun, children can learn "over and under" weaving on a strong mesh orange or onion bag which has been thumbtacked to an old picture frame. Remnants of colored yarn or string are perfect for weaving.

❁

Introduce sewing to a young child without the danger of pricked fingers by tying a piece of brightly colored gift ribbon to the loop of a bobby pin; stitching can be done on a double layer of tissue paper.

❁

A treasured gift for a child need not be an expensive one: Wrap up a package containing a large scrapbook, a jar of library paste and a collection of old magazines that are a good source of pictures to cut out.

❊

A good way to avoid torn or fingermarked snapshots is to give young children their own picture albums, keeping the best shots for the family album and turning over the rest to the children.

❊

Make a bowling set from plastic bleach bottles. Clean six bottles and paint them bright colors. Add a large plastic ball and watch the fun begin.

❊

Instead of throwing out a battered old chest of drawers, transform it into a child's dollhouse: Remove a drawer or two (for a one- or two-story house); paint the dresser, complete with windows; and move in the miniature furniture. Use the remaining drawers to store toys and doll clothes.

❊

Make flowerpots for a dollhouse from toothpaste tube caps. Fill caps with modeling clay and "plant" with small straw or artificial flowers.

❊

A doll hat and muff can be made inexpensively from fake-fur earmuffs. As the fur is already attached to elastic, one earmuff serves as the hat. To make the muff, fold the remaining earmuff in half; stitch on the wrong side.

❀

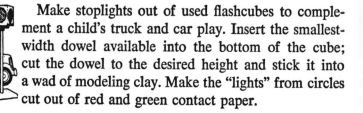

Make stoplights out of used flashcubes to complement a child's truck and car play. Insert the smallest-width dowel available into the bottom of the cube; cut the dowel to the desired height and stick it into a wad of modeling clay. Make the "lights" from circles cut out of red and green contact paper.

❀

When children outgrow squeaky rubber toys, make puppets from them. Cut them off a little below the neck and glue or sew on a piece of gathered material.

❀

As a special gift for a young child, make a map of the neighborhood with streets, familiar landmarks and houses painted in bright colors on a 3' x 4' sheet of plywood. A child will spend many happy hours pushing cars to friends' houses, boats on rivers and trains along tracks. (Lettering street names and house numbers makes it into an educational toy.)

❀

To display model planes, use a discarded lampshade frame suspended from a ceiling light fixture in a youngster's room. Attach the planes with fine wire or cord in varying lengths.

Kids' Catchall

Use a small, inflatable soft plastic wading pool as a playpen. It's easy to move from room to room and will keep the child safely within bounds; later, it can be used for its original purpose.

❀

Let children exchange pets that are not emotionally attached to families: Set up a "swap system" that includes care and feeding information as well. Before a pet leaves the house—whether it be a small hamster, a snake, white mice or numerous goldfish, make sure the person taking it is definitely interested and will provide a good home. Children are fascinated with the exchange program, and seem to take a greater responsibility for the pets.

❀

To make a work space the right height and size for a child who wants to help in the kitchen, pull out a drawer and lay a cutting board on top of it.

❀

Help a small child to turn light switches on and off by himself: Cut a rectangular hole near one end of a long cardboard tube; the hole hooks onto the switch; the tube pushes the switch up or down.

❀

When a doorknob is not within a child's reach, re-
lease the catch and nail an empty spool to the door
at the appropriate level.

❀

Children are often thrilled with simple gift items,
such as a lock and key and other hardware, or office
supplies, such as paper clips, staplers, rubber bands,
gummed labels and paper punchers.

❀

Make a family tree on a child's bedroom wall.
Paint a tree on the wall; tape family snapshots to its
branches.

❀

Economize on wallpaper for children's bedrooms.
Buy a roll of self-adhesive vinyl; cut out figures appropriate to the child's age and interests. Measure the
placement of each figure on the wall; mark with a
pencil; press the figures into place.

11.

For Those in Need

Sick Children

When a child must be hospitalized, help pass the time by writing a book together about his stay. Take photographs of the child, his room, the doctors and nurses. Have him compose a story about each photograph. Compile the photos and stories into a book.

❀

As neither hospitals nor doctors will treat a child without written permission of a parent or legal guardian, parents should write such a letter and keep it in the house. Simply state that you are the legal guardian of the children—include their names—and that you give permission for emergency help to be rendered by a licensed physician. Get a notary public to witness the signature. Make certain each child knows where the letter is kept.

❀

Give a hospitalized child a present that will help him look forward to each day. Gift-wrap a large box. Inside, put small, individually wrapped surprises, one for each day of his stay. As the box empties, he will have the additional excitement of knowing it will soon be time to go home.

❀

When children are sick at home, give them the company and attention they demand—as well as getting your own work done—by taking chores into the sickroom: Clean out the child's closets and dresser drawers, write letters, iron clothes, mend or read.

❀

Give a sick child a dinner bell to call for assistance.

❀

When a young child is sick, put a full-length mirror at the foot of the bed: The mirror will provide an audience and a source of pleasant distraction.

❀

Use this grooming tip when young children are sick with colds and flu: Each day, wash and, when possible, sun-dry combs and brushes. Then comb and brush the sick one's hair to keep it free from that oily, limp look. A little cologne on the brush makes the scalp and hair fresh and fragrant.

❀

Let a child apply stinging medication himself: His pleasure in performing the grown-up task will lessen his displeasure.

❀

Give a child an hourglass to watch while his temperature is being taken: He will be so intrigued while watching the sand that he will forget his panic.

❀

When a young child needs to be taught to gargle, try this trick: With the child watching, try to sing his favorite song while gargling. Let the child join in for the second round, with medicated fluid—a messy teaching technique, but one that works.

❀

When a child balks at taking liquid medication, try this: Mix medication with orange juice and serve in a brightly colored plastic glass, with a straw.

❀

Let a bedridden child pass the time enjoyably by cutting out pictures of fruits and vegetables from an old seed catalogue; you can use them as labels for next season's canning.

❀

When thumb-sucking threatens to lead to dental damage, cover the child's hands with puppets: With a felt-tip pen, draw faces on old socks; cover each hand with a puppet for naps and at bedtime. (This also can be used to keep children from scratching chicken pox.)

The Elderly and the Handicapped

If your household includes an old typewriter no longer used, give it to an elderly stroke patient whose writing hand has become paralyzed. Few older persons learn to write with the opposite hand; with the hunt and peck system, however, either hand can be used to type.

❀

One of the most thoughtful gifts that can be given to a woman in a nursing home is the promise of an occasional new hairdo. Anyone who can wash and set her own hair could offer this gift. It might also be done by members of a service club or a women's club.

❀

Some favorite gifts for those in nursing homes are: small plastic or fabric shopping bags; postage stamps; stationery and note paper; colored felt-tip pens; emery boards; clear nail polish; magnifying mirrors; dimes for phone calls; and lollipops for young visitors.

❀

As a Christmas or birthday present, give a "Home-made-Cookie-of-the-Month Club" certificate to someone in a nursing home.

❀

As institutions for the sick and elderly are often deluged with homemade goodies at holiday times, have your club or church organization plan to give its donations at other times of the year. The gifts will be better appreciated—and club members will be less busy—during the "off-season."

❀

Save divided TV-dinner trays and put your family's leftovers in the sections; wrap in foil and freeze. The home-cooked dinners make nice surprises for the elderly and confined.

❀

Volunteer a few hours' time on a spring Saturday to help an elderly neighbor spruce up the house: Recruit children to cut grass and weed the flower garden; wash windows, do small repairs and even paint the house if necessary. In addition to improving the looks of the neighborhood, it will boost everyone's spirits tremendously.

❀

For confirmed gardeners who are now confined to nursing homes, give a windowsill garden: Potted vegetables such as cherry tomatoes and miniature corn and peas will do well in a sunny window.

❀

Set up a weekly reading group for elderly neighbors with failing sight. A notice on the library's or the church's bulletin board is a good advertisement. Side benefits: new friendships among senior citizens, and the possibility for high school or college students to earn pocket money if a small fee is charged.

❀

Those who are too deaf to hear the telephone or doorbell can try this solution: Keep a stack of self-addressed postal cards on hand. When writing an invitation that requires a reply, enclose one of the self-addressed postal cards in the envelope. If the friend cannot keep the date you designated, he can write down his own day and hour and send it to you. Neither of you will have to worry about missing each other because of your hearing defect.

❀

Try using a swivel chair instead of a walker. The chair will allow you to go places inaccessible with a walker, and turning around is easier in the chair.

❀

As lap robes tend to slip and slide, make a "lap apron" for a person confined to a wheelchair: Leave the blanket full length in front; shorten the side pieces to hang from the waist to the chair seat and cut them so that they curve upward (to avoid entanglement in wheelchair spokes). Add a sash, so that the garment can be tied around the waist. Lastly, add cobbler's-apron-type pockets to the front, to hold such items as glasses, tissues, books and pills.

Hospital Patients

Double reachable space for the bedridden by putting a lazy Susan on the nightstand.

❀

To groom the hair of the bedridden, put an old stocking over a hairbrush. Dandruff and oil will cling to the stocking.

❀

As a cheery addition to the sickroom, make a miniature garden in a brandy snifter or other glass container: Dig up a small clump of flowering plants—violets, for example—roots and all; add a bit of green moss or small pebbles at the base of the plant. Water lightly. Miniature insect or animal figures can be added to complete the scene.

❀

A divider tray for kitchen utensils makes a good gift for someone in the hospital: It provides a place to store such things as toiletries, stamps, stationery, pens, etc.

❀

Give a hospitalized person gaily flowered pillowcases as an alternative to flowers.

❀

Instead of ordering one large floral arrangement for a hospitalized friend or relative, pick out a bud vase and ask the florist to deliver it with one rosebud, and to send a fresh rosebud every third day.

❀

Arrange for a manicurist to visit a friend or relative in the hospital.

❀

When choosing a gift for someone in the hospital, give a "forward-looking" gift—something that the person will be able to use once he is well and at home again.

❀

Do not neglect those hospitalized for emotional problems: At such times cards, flowers and visits are often a reassuring link to society.

Medical Catchall

For a sore throat, gargle with hot salt water.

❀

Lightly butter pills for people who have trouble swallowing them—the pill will go down even before the patient has lifted his water glass.

❀

Before removing a splinter or a thorn, hold an ice cube on the spot.

❀

Freeze wet washcloths in plastic sandwich bags. They are instant help for bumps and bruises; can be used to numb splinter areas for painless removal; and are excellent help for minor burns—hold on burn until pain stops.

❀

Keep a plaster leg or arm cast dry while showering by covering it with a large garbage-can liner; use water-resistant electrical or plastic tape to keep the liner in place.

❀

Keep medicine that must be stored in the refrigerator out of the hands of children by placing it in a large jar with a cap too wide for little hands to grip and open.

12.

Personal Hygiene
and Grooming Tips

Use a small pocket calculator to count calories throughout the day. It's much easier than writing down everything and then adding it up at the end of the day; and it ensures that the dieter will be aware of reaching the limit of the diet before it is too late.

❀

Keep hands soft by rinsing them with vinegar water after hand-washing clothes or dishes.

❀

Give yourself a relaxing facial sauna: Cut out the bottom and part of one side of a plastic, gallon-size milk or bleach jug, copying the shape of the shield of a store-bought sauna. Place the jug upside down in a baby-bottle warmer, add water and plug in. An economical luxury, a facial sauna at home does marvelous things for the complexion.

❀

To banish yellow from white hair—on humans as well as dogs—mix 2 tablespoons of liquid laundry bluing with 2½ quarts lukewarm water. After shampooing and rinsing, pour the solution over the hair, being careful to keep it out of eyes and ears, count to ten, and rinse. Repeat the process when necessary.

❀

When hair is dirty but washing must be postponed, use an old-fashioned, quick and inexpensive method of dry shampooing: Sprinkle talcum or bath powder onto oily areas, rub vigorously with a towel, and brush out.

❀

Help yourself cut down or eliminate smoking: Instead of reaching for a cigarette when the telephone rings, sniff a beautiful rose, peony, lily of the valley or other fragrant flower.

❀

After a day at the beach, remove the last traces of sand from the body or feet by sprinkling on talcum powder and rubbing lightly with a towel. The sand will vanish as if by magic.

❀

For troubled complexions, a good, inexpensive home remedy is to rub baby powder or cornstarch on the face after cleaning. This dries pimples without drying skin.

❀

A turned-over dinner plate makes an ideal hand rest for applying fingernail polish.

❀

Mix the last bit of lipstick thoroughly with cold cream and you'll have a lovely, creamy rouge.

❀

Avoid struggling to remove shoe polish from under fingernails by assigning a pair of worn-out gloves to your shoe-polishing kit.

13.

Money Matters and Budgeting

Using a copying machine, keep a visual record of wallet contents—credit cards, driver's license, charge plates, etc.—on a sheet of paper to insure prompt and accurate reporting in case of loss or theft.

❀

As an extra precaution, write your name, address, telephone number and bicycle serial number on a file card, roll the card into a tight cylinder, take off the bicycle seat and drop the card into the frame. Even though the thief may have filed off the serial number, the card can easily be retrieved and used as proof of ownership.

❀

Tape vital telephone numbers, for police, fire department, doctor, etc., to the cradle of the phone under the receiver.

❀

Keep a "want list" on the back of the kitchen door to monitor impulsive spending. Each family member lists whatever items he would most like to have. At the end of each month let a different member of the family select one item from the list.

❀

Make a "Day of Reckoning" box—any type of box will do—for your kitchen. Put all receipts, bills and notes on household expenses into the box for easy reference at the end of the month when you do your accounting. This will save time—no more hunting in nooks and crannies for necessary information.

❀

Curb impulsive spending by deciding on one "surprise" per payday. Draw a sketch of the item, or print the words on a slip of paper, and paper clip it to the amount of dollar bills necessary to buy the item. The reminder in your wallet will help in resisting other items.

❀

Repaying a large loan from a friend or relative by installments is easier if a savings account is taken out in the lender's name and regular deposits are made into the account each payday.

❀

If eating out is a pleasure but strains the family budget, eat weekend breakfasts out—the cost is considerably less than a dinner.

❀

Earn pocket money by creating your own part-time job as the neighborhood errand runner. For a modest fee, return borrowed items, mail letters, drop off library books, deliver gifts, etc. Announce the service at the local women's club; work out schedules the day before with those who enlist your help.

❀

To raise funds for church or community, send each member a dollar bill to be put to work for the common good, i.e., to generate more money. Be ingenious. For example, invest in seeds for cucumbers: After harvesting, make dill pickles, pack them in quart jars and charge a dollar a quart. Put your craft skills to work. Set a time limit of about four months (June to September) and give a fund-raising party to sell the results.

�֎

Set up a school store in August for two weeks, from 10:00 A.M. to noon, to sell books and supplies the children need for the coming year.

�֎

Join together with neighbors to purchase major power tools for the lawn: mower, hedge clippers, lawn edgers and lawn sweepers. Each family participating should pay an equal share of costs, with priority weeks for each established at the beginning. During each family's priority weeks, other families who want to use the tools can rent the equipment when it is not in use. The rental fees can be put into a fund for repairs and replacements. Bookkeeping can be rotated. This plan can be so successful that groups might use it to buy simple carpentry tools.

✖

When handling new paper money, which tends to stick together, avoid the possibility of handing out two bills instead of one by reversing them in your billfold—putting one face up, the next face down, etc.

14.

Miscellaneous Hints

A thoughtful gift from previous tenants for new homeowners is a "Get-Acquainted Kit" left behind on the kitchen table. It should include a local telephone book; the names and addresses of the closest neighbors along with the ages of their children; a list of the police and fire department numbers; a local map; all the manuals of the remaining appliances; and a quick sketch of the shrubs and plants on the grounds, with all their common names.

❀

Children five years old and up will happily anticipate a distant move if they see in advance photographs of their new house and of the local school, library, fire station, service station, supermarket and other landmarks.

❀

Be sure to take a local telephone book along when the family makes a major move. It will be an invaluable reference for many months after arriving in the new home. New family doctors need names and addresses of former doctors; department stores ask for at least three credit card references, complete with addresses; new schools want names and addresses of former schools for records; Christmas card lists and hospital greetings can be prepared without delay. A real time-saver!

❀

When odd jobs remain ignored in an all-too-crowded day, stay up ten minutes longer than you usually would and do them before going to bed. This little time span gives you an opportunity to: paste recipes and poems into scrapbooks and snapshots into albums; write letters; clip favorite stories from magazines; wrap presents; address greeting cards; etc.

❀

An effective way to cut down on electricity bills is to remind family members to turn off the cellar light by printing the word "LIGHT" in white paint on the upright area of your top cellar step; anyone coming up will be sure to see it.

❀

Take the telephone receiver off the hook when taking a bath or shower: People will know you are home and will call again, saving you a mad dash to the phone.

❀

Perk up matted artificial fur by brushing with a wire pet brush.

❀

When opening a new box of facial tissues, cut tissues in half: They will still be large enough for most uses, and will go twice as far.

❀

Make emergency raincoats by slitting holes for arms and heads in large plastic trash-can liners.

❀

Before carrying heavy items in a paper shopping bag, place a cardboard shoe box at the bottom of the bag for reinforcement; this will also ensure that the bag will stay upright when you set it down.

❀

When a baby reaches the crawling stage, cover the tips of his shoes with adhesive tape to keep them from becoming scruffy.

❀

Glue an address label to a spring-type clothespin and use it to clip shoes or overshoes together when they must be left with many others of a similar kind. This is especially helpful to schoolchildren for identifying their shoes.

❀

Use a cotton swab dipped in bleach to mark children's names in the insides of boots.

❀

Apply adhesive tape to the inside of sandal straps to lengthen the life of the shoe.

❀

Insert the hose of a hairdryer into boots to dry them quickly.

❀

To help boots hold their shape, stand large soft-drink bottles inside them.

❀

Hang boots from a skirt hanger and they will lose their creases.

❀

Repair rubber boots with an inner-tube repair kit, which can be bought inexpensively at hardware stores.

❀

Keep books borrowed from friends clean by covering them in brown wrapping paper. As a reminder to return the book, write the owner's name and the date when the book was borrowed on the cover.

❀

When book jackets become worn, cut out the information about the author from the jacket and paste it on the flyleaf; also keep articles about favorite authors and interesting reviews in your copies of their books.

❀

To make a bookmark, cut the corner off an envelope and split it over the corner of the page.

❀

Save money on magazine subscriptions by setting up a neighborhood rotating system. Each family subscribes to two periodicals; when everyone is finished rotating monthly magazines, take turns delivering them to local hospitals or nursing homes.

❀

Make a game of cleaning up the neighborhood: Send children on a scavenger hunt in a given area to hunt for refuse. Assign cans a value of three points, unbroken bottles two points and papers one point. Give one prize or a group party at the end of the hunt.

❀

To insure that puppies or kittens each receive their proper share of food, set out the portions in a muffin tin. The animals will fall into natural litter formation.

❀

Try this trick for housebreaking a puppy: Hang a bell by a rubber band—so that it bounces—from a doorknob. Each time the puppy is taken outside to "perform," ring the bell. Within a few days he will be able to tell *you* when he needs to go out.

❀

During winter, keep ice balls from forming between the toes and pads of a dog's feet by carefully trimming the hair from the area.

❀

Put reflector tape on the family pet's collar. This may prevent its being run over at night.

❀

In households where someone repeatedly forgets or loses his key, try this trick: Put an extra key along with the license tag on the family dog's collar. (This works best when dog is a loud watchdog.)

❀

Trade spare keys with trusted neighbors to prevent getting locked out of the home. Put the spare in a hiding place in the neighbor's yard—under a rock or wherever best hidden.

❀

Keep your change in a bright red coin purse to prevent frantic searching in your handbag; it shows up even when the light is poor and can be picked out easily from the "flotsam and jetsam."

❀

When mailing fragile items, put them in plastic bags and surround with marshmallows.

❀

For pasting stamps and sealing envelopes, use an empty roll-on-deodorant bottle filled with water.

❀

If postage stamps have stuck together, put them in the freezer for fifteen minutes; they will come apart easily.

❀

Keep stamped postcards on hand for sending opinions to senators and congressmen. They do tabulate their mail and vote with the consensus of their constituents.

❀

Fasten a tiny flashlight to a large plastic kite for night flying.

❀

Those with swimming pools can save water and money spent on water bills, by catching rain: Simply attach an elbow conection to the downspouts of house gutters. When it begins to rain, let dirt and dust be washed from the roof for the first few minutes; as soon as the water begins to run clean, stick a length of pipe into the elbow connection and run the pipe to the pool. The pool filter will do any necessary additional cleaning.

❀

Use an adjustable ironing board as a typing table for a small, light machine. It allows a more comfortable height for a variety of people.

❀ ❀

Index

Anniversaries, 151
Art, children and, 196-197, 202

Baby showers, 143-144
Bathing children, 183
Bird watching, backyard, 104-106
Birthdays, 145-148
Breads, 65-67
Bridal showers, 148-150
Budgeting, 219-220
Butter, 68-69

Cakes, 78-81
Camping, 165-166
  cooking at the campsite, 167-168
Car hints, 163-164
Cheese, 69
Children
  art and, 196-197, 202
  bathing, 183
  birthdays and, 145-148
  catchall ideas for, 201-202
  Christmas and, 152-155
  clothes, recycling of, 118-122
  clothes and accessories, storage of, 33-36
  dressing, 184-185, 227
  Easter and, 155-156

eating, 179-181
encouraging play, 193-195
family harmony (togetherness), 173-179
gifts and
  decorating, 159
  holiday gift-giving, 152-155
  wrapping, 159-160
grooming, 183-184
Halloween and, 156
housecleaning and, 16
learning and, 188-192
money, the value of, and, 192-193
moving with, 225
pets and, 201, 229
room organization and storage, 38-40
safety and, 186-187
schoolwork, 188-192
sickness and, 205-207
sleeping, 181-182
toys to make, 197-200
traveling with, 168-170
Christmas, 152-155
  holiday gift-giving, 152-155
Cleaning and housework, 15-30
  curtains, 24-25
  defrosting, 50-52

Cleaning and housework
(*cont.*)
dishwashing, 50-52
general data on, 15-17, 28-
30
laundry
drying, 18-20
ironing, 21-23
washing, 18-20
odors, removal of, 26-28
spots, removal of, 26-28
stains, removal of, 26-28
upholstery, 25-26
walls, 24
windows, 24
Clean-up catchall, 28-30
Clothes
accessories and, storage of,
33-36
recycling, 118-122
Cookies, 81-82
Cooking techniques, 52-57
cooking at the campsite,
167-168
See also Food ideas
Crafts, 135-139
Crocheting, 128-131
Curtains, cleaning, 24-25

Decorating gifts, 159-160
Decorating ideas, 135-139
Defrosting, 50-52
Desserts
cakes, 78-81
cookies, 81-82
fruits, 75-78
general data on, 83-84
leftovers, 83

cakes, 79-80
fruits, 76
pies, 82-83
Dishwashing, 50-52
Dressing children, 184-185,
227
Drying laundry, 18-20

Easter, 155-156
Eating, children and, 179-
181
Eggs, 67-68
Elderly, the, gifts for, 208-
210
Embroidery, 125-127

Family harmony (together-
ness), 173-179
Fish, 58-59, 62
Flowers, indoor, 95-98
Food ideas, 58-83
breads, 65-67
butter, 68-69
cakes, 78-81
cheese, 69
cookies, 81-82
cooking techniques, 52-57
cooking at the campsite,
167-168
desserts
cakes, 78-81
cookies, 81-82
fruits, 75-78
general data on, 83-84
pies, 82-83
eggs, 67-68
fish, 58-59, 62
fruits, 75-78

grain, 67
meats, 58-60
pies, 82-83
potatoes, 63-64
poultry, 60-62
    general data on, 58-60
rice, 64-65
salads, 74-75
vegetables, 69-74
See also Leftovers
Fruits, 75-78

Gardening, outdoor, 98-104
Gifts, 152-155
    children and holiday gift-
        giving, 152-155
    decorating, 159-160
    for the elderly, 208-210
    general hints for, 157-158
    for the handicapped, 207,
        209-210
    for hospital patients, 210-
        211
    wrapping, 159-160
Grains, 67
Grooming, 215-216
    children and, 183-184

Halloween, 156
Handicapped, the, gifts for,
    207, 209-210
Home repairs, 88-92
    general data on, 88-92
    painting, 87-88
    plastering, 88
Hospital patients, gifts for,
    210-211

Household hints, miscel-
    laneous, 225-230
Housework, general, 15-17
    See also Cleaning and
        housework
Hygiene, personal, 215-216

Indoor flowers, 95-98
Indoor plants, 95-98
Ironing, 21-23

Kitchen
    defrosting, 50-52
    dishwashing, 50-52
    general data on, 47-52
    organization and storage
        in, 36-38, 47-50
    See also Cooking tech-
        niques; Food ideas
Knitting, 127-130

Laundry
    drying, 18-20
    ironing, 21-23
    washing, 18-20
Learning, children and, 188-
    192
Leftovers
    bread, 65-67
        garlic, 59
    cake, 79-80
    desserts, 83
        cakes, 79-80
        fruits, 76
    eggs, 62
    fruits, 76
    hamburgers, 64
    hash, 58

Leftovers (*cont.*)
lamb, 59
meatballs, 58
omelet from, 68
potatoes
mashed, 63
salad, 64
poultry, 62
tuna fish, 62
vegetables, 59, 70, 71
waffles, 66

Meat, general data on, 58-60
Medical aids, 211-212
Mending techniques, 115-118
Miscellaneous household hints, 225-230
Money
budgeting and other matters, 219-220
children and learning the value of, 192-193
Motor trips, 163-164
Moving, children and, 225

Needlework, 125-135
crocheting, 128-131
embroidery, 125-127
knitting, 127-130
patchwork, 131-133
quilting, 131-133
rugmaking, 133-135
thread, 125-127
yarn, 125-127
New arrivals, 143-144

Odors, removal of, 26-28

Organization and storage, 33-43
in the children's rooms, 38-40
clothing and accessories, 33-36
around the house, 40-43
in the kitchen, 36-38, 47-50
Outdoor gardening, 98-104

Painting, 87-88
Parties, general hints for, 157
Patchwork, 131-133
Personal hygiene, 215-216
Pets, children and, 201, 229
Pies, 82-83
Plants, indoor, 95-98
Plastering, 88
Play, encouraging children to, 193-195
Potatoes, 63-64
Poultry, 60-62
general data on, 58-60

Quilting, 131-133

Recycling clothes, 118-122
Rice, 64-65
Rugmaking, 133-135

Safety, children and, 186-187
Salads, 74-75
Schoolwork, children and, 188-192
Sewing, 109-122
clothes, recycling, 118-122

general data on, 109-118
mending techniques, 115-118
Shopping, 47-50
Showers
  baby, 143-144
  bridal, 148-150
Sickness, children and, 205-207
Sleeping, children and, 181-182
Special occasions
  anniversaries, 151
  baby showers, 143-144
  birthdays, 145-148
  bridal showers, 148-150
  Christmas, 152-155
  Easter, 155-156
  gifts and, 152-155
    children and holiday gift-giving, 152-155
    decorating, 159
    for the elderly, 208-210
    general hints, 157-158
    for the handicapped, 207, 209-210
    for hospital patients, 210-211
    wrapping, 159-160
  Halloween, 156
  new arrivals, 143-144

parties, general hints for, 157
  weddings, 150-151
Spots, removal of, 26-28
Stains, removal of, 26-28
Storage, *see* Organization and storage

Thread, 125-127
Toy making, children and, 197-200
Traveling, 163-170
  camping, 165-166
    cooking at the campsite, 167-168
  car hints, 163-164
  with children, 168-170
  motor trip hints, 163-164

Upholstery, cleaning, 25-26

Vegetables, 69-74

Walls, cleaning, 24
Washing laundry, 18-20
Weddings, 150-151
Windows, cleaning, 24
Wrapping gifts, 159-160

Yarn, 125-127